DIGITAL ECONOMY
&
DIRECT TAXATION

DIGITAL ECONOMY & DIRECT TAXATION

An Overview

2022

K R Sekar

Foreword by
Parthasarathi Shome
Chairman, International Tax Research and Analysis Foundation

ITRAF
INTERNATIONAL TAX RESEARCH AND ANALYSIS FOUNDATION

OakBridge

Published by
OakBridge Publishing Pvt. Ltd.
M 35, 1st Floor, Old DLF, Gurugram, 122001, Haryana, India
Tel.: +91 124 4305970, E-mail: info@oakbridge.in
www.oakbridge.in

ISBN: 978-93-91032-68-5

Printed and bound at Saurabh Printers Pvt.Ltd.

Dedicated to my Living God and Guru
Sri Kanchi Kamakoti Sankarcharya
Sri Sankara Vijayendra Saraswathi

Foreword

The digitisation of economic activity has been posing challenges in taxing jurisdictions reflecting its global reach. The ability to connect any smart device to a network of networks has enabled an "internet of things". They comprise a series of components of equal importance including machine-to-machine communication, cloud computing, big data analysis, sensors and actuators, the combination of which leads to further developments in machine learning and remote control. The number of devices connected to the Internet is expanding rapidly, but it is miniscule in terms of potential. As increasing numbers of connected devices are developed and sold, machine-to-machine communication should expand and improve the ability and efficiency of businesses to collect and analyse data.[1]

Virtual currencies are digital units of exchange that are not yet backed by government-issued legal tender, though China is already using it. They can be used in online games to purchase in-game assets and services. In some cases, they can be exchanged for real currencies or used to purchase real goods and services, through exchanges that may be operated by the game creators or by third parties. Other virtual currencies also exist, for example, cryptocurrencies, including bitcoins. They rely on peer-to-peer verification to secure and verify transactions. Some private operators are accepting payment in bitcoins.

Advanced robotics are robots that are making manufacturing more efficient and productive through the use of automated factories. Multinational enterprises (MNEs) can take advantage of lower labour costs and move to where their customers are. Three-dimensional (3D) printing also brings manufacturing closer to the customer, with direct interaction with them to design product features. Manufacturing could gradually move away from mass production to customised products, and more experimentation.

In 2011, the OECD defined digital economy that uses e-commerce as,

> the sale or purchase of goods or services, conducted over computer networks by methods specifically designed for the purpose of receiving or placing of orders. The goods or services are ordered by those methods, but the payment and the ultimate delivery of the goods or service do not have to be conducted online. An e-commerce transaction can be between enterprises, households, individuals, governments, and other public or private organisations.

---

1. Shome, Parthasarathi. 2021. *Taxation History, Theory, Law and Administration*. Springer Texts in Business and Economics. Cham: Springer. https://doi.org/10.1007/978-3-030-68214-9.

Reflecting the rapid development of complexity, digitalisation has exacerbated base erosion and profit shifting (BEPS) possibilities by multinational enterprises and raised a series of broader tax challenges related to how taxing rights on income generated from cross-border activities in the digital age should be allocated among jurisdictions. The matter has been taken up rapidly from the OECD's 2013 BEPS Action Plan, the October 2015 Action 1 Final Report on the digital economy, as well as continuing discussions and debates thereafter observed that associated "nexus, data and characterisation" issues were identified, but there was no agreement or recommendation in the Action 1 report. The G20 asked that OECD's multilateral Inclusive Framework (IF) of more than 100 countries deliver a consensus-based solution to the tax challenges of the digital economy by 2020.

The IF released a Policy Note in January 2019 that grouped proposals into two pillars - one on nexus and profit allocation (Pillar 1) and one on ensuring a minimum level of taxation (Pillar 2). Pillar 1 did not generate consensus; hence the OECD developed a "Unified Approach" (UA) to build on the commonalities identified. It released it for public comment in October 2019. A public consultation was held also on Pillar 2 in December 2019. In January 2020, the IF reiterated its commitment to the two-pillar approach, issuing a note entitled, "Outline of the Architecture of a Unified Approach on Pillar One", with 11 building blocks for a solution. A progress note on Pillar 2 was also agreed. Unfortunately, in mid-October 2020, the OECD issued a statement essentially indicating that the work had stalled and that it was deferring the discussions for an IF on Pillar One discussions.

In August 2020, the United Nations released an alternative framework for taxing the digital economy though it did not generate immediate traction.

Thus, the taxation of digital services continues to be sensitive with mainly the United States at odds with the international community. In its absence, emerging and advanced economies alike have taken unilateral steps to tax it against which the US has begun taken legal steps through their own domestic institutions.

What has given rise to such complexity in multilateral discussions and the failure to arrive at any agreement to develop international norms for the taxation of the digital economy? It is essential to comprehend the digital economy in its operational nature and technical characteristics, followed by the challenges encountered in arriving at a multilateral consensus regarding how to tax it. This is what K R Sekar's volume sets out to do.

Challenges in the taxation of the digital economy in the context of its new business models comprise: (i) identification of significant economic and digital presence; (ii) avoiding the creation of permanent establishment (PE) status;

(iii) attribution of profits to PE or a significant economic presence; (iv) application of transfer pricing (TP) to new business models; and (v) collection of tax.

Tax treaties allocate the right to tax profits if a PE or business connection/nexus is established, though royalties have no such pre-requisite. There is a significant difference in the rate of tax levied-40 percent for business income and 10 percent on royalty, in the case of India. Thus, disputes arise, for example, over the characterisation of income from subscription fee, whether it is business income or royalty. Tax authorities tend to characterize it as business income to maximise tax liability while businesses attempt to minimise it by characterising it as royalty. Further, given that a PE has a geographical connection, it does not fit well into the digital landscape which cuts across geographies. Since a digital enterprise may not require personnel to be placed locally, arm's length price (ALP) based on functions performed, remains a challenge for PE type calculations.

India imposed a 6 percent Equalisation Levy (EL) on digital transactions in 2016. Its scope was widened in 2020 while lowering the rate to 2%. The widely worded provision should technically cover online transactions ranging from hotel bookings and software purchases to even buying certain components from overseas. It is applicable to considerations received or receivable by non-resident (NR) e-commerce operators, and so might have a substantial impact on the business models of ecommerce giants such as Walmart-owned Flipkart, Amazon and Club Factory.[2] The US views the EL and other prevailing digital economy taxes as ring-fencing the digital economy. From the Office of the U.S. Trade Representative (USTR) initiated investigations into global instances of EL's concluding (in the case of France) that they were unreasonable, unfair and discriminatory towards U.S. commerce, and cautioned that retaliatory high tariffs of as high as 25 percent would be imposed. The events continue to unfold. Such countries need to weigh their revenue needs against the increased post-tariff product prices at market entry and the associated decrease in the international competitiveness of domestic firms on whom the burden of US tariffs would fall. While an increasingly fractured structure of digital taxes and commodity counter-tariffs seems to be here to stay for the foreseeable future.

In light of this, Sekar's volume begins with the evolution and global trends of the digital economy and its business models including blockchain and bitcoins, proceeding to its BEPS that has emerged in particular in this century. He examines country responses including the use of 'significant economic presence' by India to establish taxability, how nexus-based permanent establishment may be defined

2. Shome, P. (ed.). 2021. *Reimagining International Taxation*. Gurugram: ITRAF and Oakbridge Publishers.

in this context, taxation possibilities of bitcoins and a range of related considerations. He then describes the Indian experience in these matters including Supreme Court ruling, the EL and the recent expansion of its scope in 2020. He examines international developments in multilateral agreements and their impact on India. He covers a range of aspects of the OECD's Pillar 1 and Pillar 2 discussions on digital economy taxation and minimum tax followed by instances of international case law.

The International Tax Research and Analysis Foundation (ITRAF) is glad to have sponsored Sekar's research on digital economy taxation. The effort has resulted in a comprehensive volume on the digital economy and its taxation. Tax professionals will find it of interest to read and draw conclusions in this field from a perusal of it.

Parthasarathi Shome
Chairman, ITRAF
Bangalore

Preface

The method of doing business has undergone a significant change in recent times. Up till the 1980s, businesses were being conducted on a brick and mortar model. This entailed physical manufacturing and physical sale of goods through agents/distributors. Consequently, the taxation rules that developed were primarily around Permanent Establishment on the basis of fixed place of business or agency business. In addition, considering the way the business was being carried on in the developed countries the taxation rules were more favourably inclined towards residence based taxation and the taxation of profits was based on a simple transfer pricing method.

In the late 1980s and 1990s, the service sector gained prominence and the developing countries wanted to earn tax on profits through services rendered. The developing economies sought to tax profits through the attribution rule on the possibility of creating a Service PE. The developing economies identified a threshold for creation of service PE and also sought to charge a Withholding Tax on services through Fees for Technical Services.

With technological advancements and the emergence of digital businesses, application of conventional rules of taxation posed multiple challenges owing to the non-applicability of rules of PE to the new method of doing business. This also led to increase in disputes relating to taxation of digital businesses.

Of late the Digital Business Model has taken precedence over all other business models. Under the Digital Economy, the source of manufacturing, place of export or import etc have become redundant and the application of taxation principles to such businesses has led to multiple challenges and an inherent conflict among multiple economies. The economies plan to adopt a new approach called "Market based approach" to tax profits arising out of the Digital Economy. The fundamental principle of taxation of profits on the basis of sale and consequent allocation of profits on the basis of Functional Asset and Risk analysis of Manufacturing and Sale is posing several complications in its application. Consequent to this the Separate Entity approach which is the cornerstone of attribution of profits as enshrined in Article 7(1) of the Model Convention is not being accepted by various economies, thus leading to enforcement of "source based taxation" principle on the business carried in the respective countries.

The recent pronouncements by OECD on Alternative Model on Pillar 1 and Pillar 2 and also on the various issues connected to source basis of taxation seeks to overcome the challenge related to attribution of profits in Digital Economy. The moot point whether this is the right tax architecture is a matter of debate and I am of the view that entire Pillar 1 and Pillar 2 approach is highly debatable and the countries may find it difficult to implement it, as every country seeks to maximise the tax collection on the income sourced from its country. India's introduction of Equalisation levy and the consequent disapproval by USTR on India's Equalisation levy is a classic example of conflict on collection of taxes between two important trade partners. In my view the Pillar 1 and Pillar 2 may pose serious issues and countries may disapprove the approach of other country. The taxation of software and taxation of PE due to services rendered in the past is a classic example of how each country devised their own rules of taxation on such payments.

Further, the reluctance of some of the countries to enforce Arbitration and Conciliation as a method of resolving disputes may lead to further challenges. It is always said "Taxation rules follows the business" and taxation of Digital Economy is not an exception.

In light of the above it is important that taxation and economic professionals should come with an alternative architecture which is acceptable as well as simple in its application with minimal disputes.

Against this backdrop I have made an attempt to identify direct tax issues relating to Digital Economy with an intent to give an overview of various provisions along with a macro-outlook on some of the recent proposals. This publication is intended to serve as a summary and analysis of key aspects and highlights the challenges faced in implementation of some of the proposals.

We are also aware that OECD is finalising the approach on proposals on Pillar 1 and Pillar 2 and hence in this book I dealt on this topics only as an introduction and not as a research. I am conscious of updating this book once OECD finalizes the approach and addressing the issues and concerns of all countries on adoption of Pillar 1 and Pillar 2.

In my humble opinion to write this sort of book requires the support of organisation, colleagues and well-wishers and above all the blessings of God.

I should thank my organisation, Deloitte India, for encouraging me to be part of ITRAF (International Tax Research Analysis and Foundation) and supporting me in writing a research publication.

I would like to thank my colleagues for encouraging me with their inputs and comments. Notably Shefali, Rashmi, Priya, Ananth, Ankitha Kumari and my other colleagues. I have mentioned their names in some places as a reference.

I should thank Dr. Partho Shome, my mentor at ITRAF, who has encouraged me, advised me and more importantly has been a source of inspiration to complete this book. I am grateful to him for writing a lucid and thought-provoking foreword.

Finally, nothing is possible without the blessings of God, my parents, and my family. My parents who have departed to their heavenly abode still continue to bless me.

I need to thank my family as the family has willingly allowed me to spend time on this book which otherwise belongs to them and also for the solid support for me on any of my work beyond family.

Above all I am fortunate enough to receive the blessings of my living God and Guru His Holiness of Kanchi Kamakoti Sri Sankara Vijayendra Saraswathi and I dedicate this publication at his lotus feet and but for his blessings I would not have even made an attempt to start something on this.

September 10, 2021 **K R Sekar**
Madras

About the Author

K.R. Sekar is a Founder Member and Director on the Board of ITRAF. He is a Tax Partner with Deloitte Touche Tohmatsu India LLP. He has over 25 years of experience in the fields of direct taxes, mergers and acquisitions, international taxation and transfer pricing. His key areas of expertise include inbound structuring, litigation support and advising on cross-border tax issues. He is also associated with many landmark litigation cases for global companies. He was recognised as one of the leading Tax Controversy Leaders 2013 by International Tax Review, UK.

General Contents

Detailed Contents

ANNEXURES

Abbreviations and Acronyms

Term	Description
AAR	Authority for Advance Rulings
AI	Artificial intelligence
AR	Augmented reality
BEPS	Base erosion and profit shifting
BLA	Brand licence agreement
CBDT	Central Board of Direct Taxes
CFB	Consumer facing business
CFC	Controlled foreign corporation
CTA	Covered Tax Agreement
DAT	Digital advertising tax
DEMPE	Development, enhancement, maintenance, protection and exploitation of intangibles
DST	Digital services tax
DTA	Double taxation agreement
DTAA	Double Taxation Avoidance Agreement
EL	Equalisation levy
ERP	Enterprise resource planning
FEMA	Foreign Exchange Management Act
FinCEN	Financial Crimes Enforcement Network
FTEs	Fiscally transparent entities
FTS	Fee for technical services
GILTI	Global intangible low-taxed income
ICT	Information and communication technology
IoT	Internet of things
IP	Internet protocol
ISPA	India sale purchase agreement
IT/OT	Information technology/Operational technology

Term	Description
ITAT	Income tax Appellate Tribunal
ITeS	Information technology enabled services
LLPs	Limited liability partnership
LO	Liaison office
MAP	Mutual agreement procedure
ML	Machine learning
MLA	Multilateral agreements
MLE	Multi-location enterprises
MLI	Multilateral instrument
MNE	Multinational enterprise
NBFC	Non-banking financial companies
OECD	Organisation for Economic Co-operation and Development
PBT	Profit before tax
PE	Private equity
PE	Permanent establishment
POEM	Place of effective management
PPT	Principal purpose tax
PSM	Profit split method
R&D	Research and development
RBI	Reserve Bank of India
SC	Supreme Court
SEP	Significant economic presence
VAT	Value-added tax
VCs	Virtual currencies
VR	Virtual reality
WHT	Withholding tax

Chapter 1

INTRODUCTION

Evolution of Digital Economy

The digital economy — which is in a state of continuous evolution — is an upshot of the transformative process brought by the information and communication technology (ICT) revolution that has made technologies cheaper, more powerful, and widely standardised; thereby improving business processes and bolstering innovation across all sectors of the economy.

The development of ICT has been characterised by rapid technological progress, adoption, and application of low-cost technology in various industry sectors, and a concomitant fall in the prices of ICT-driven products/services. The advances in technology and the pressure to innovate have fuelled commoditisation of several key technologies, thus giving a boost to digital economy.

The ICT products and services have made tremendous progress from the days of proprietary computing hardware, which meant that the computers of different manufacturers operated in silos on different standards, protected under a patent. When the architecture of personal computers was largely standardised 30 years ago, market players started competing on price. That, combined with rapid technological progress, resulted in a substantial price cut of personal computing hardware. Today businesses are striving to standardise their products/services so as to make them vulnerable to duplication, even as digital technologies are creating new opportunities at different stages of the value chain.

Going ahead, the critical success factor for any digital product will be its ability to integrate with other products — internet of things (IoT) which is about devices, data, and connectivity — to realise the future of a smart, connected world.

The designing, manufacturing, and selling of artificial intelligence-enabled products like fitness bands, smartphones, and tablets — which seamlessly integrate packages of hardware and software — and services have allowed companies to strengthen their position across the business value chain in their markets.

In addition to product design, today businesses are using artificial intelligence (AI) to reimagine their product development life cycles and deploying machine learning (ML) algorithms to categorise work, introduce agile workflows and drive greater automation. They are also providing a plethora of e-commerce formats like apps, websites, and chatbots to enhance the overall pre- and post-sales customer experience.

In a nutshell, the digital economy is reshaping the world in unimaginable ways. The evolution of portable computing devices, faster telecommunication networks, cloud computing, as well as emerging trends like IoT and Edge, big data, AI, virtual currencies, advanced robotics, and 3D printing have all contributed towards making us a digital-first society.

Global Trends

The Organisation for Economic Co-operation and Development (OECD)[1] classifies digital trends into technology trends and digital transformation. Digital technologies are fast-accelerating technologies known for their complexity, modularity, and rapid obsolescence, for example, robotics, drones and connected cars to name a few. Between 2013 and 2016, only a few countries had contributed to the top 25 fast-accelerating digital technologies. While Japan and Korea were involved in the development of all ICT fields during this period,[2] China and the US were among the top 5 players in emerging digital technologies.

The following diagram depicts the top players in emerging digital technologies during 2013 to 2016.

1. Refer to Measuring the Digital Transformation: A Roadmap for the Future, OECD Report, 2019 ("OECD Report, 2019").
2. Page 31 of OECD Report, 2019.

1. Top players in emerging digital technologies, 2013-16

Share of top five economies' patents in top 25 technologies fast accelerating from 2010 onwards

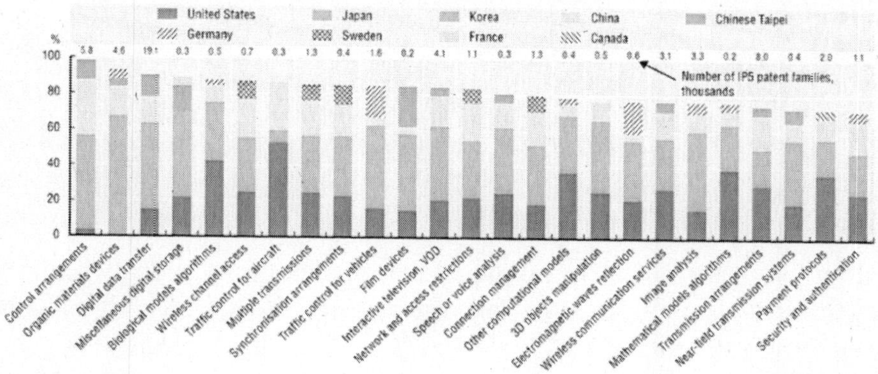

Source: OECD, STI Micro-data Lab: Intellectual Property Database, http://oe.cd/ipstats, January 2019. See chapter notes. StatLink contains more data.
StatLink https://doi.org/10.1787/888933928293

Source: Measuring the Digital Transformation: A Roadmap for the Future, OECD Report, 2019

According to the OECD Report, the key technologies that will impact and drive digital transformation are discussed below.

Artificial Intelligence

Artificial intelligence — a new technology wave that has accelerated since 2010 —is a term used to describe machines performing human-like cognitive functions (e.g., learning, understanding, reasoning, or interacting). In fact, AI is already impacting almost every industry and is the key driver of emerging technologies like big data and internet of things. Most organisations and businesses are leveraging AI to drive operational efficiency. AI is being harnessed to get real-time insights into production, forecasting, supply chain, etc. AI can also help governments address issues for instance those relating to environment, healthcare, logistics, and transportation. In 2018, there were about 6000 AI-related companies in the United Kingdom alone, according to data from Glass AI[3].

Network

The mobile network is critical to the success of digital business. Since the days of 2G, mobile connectivity has witnessed massive transformation and

3. The company that interprets open web text at scale.

improvements. 5G, now i stages of roll out, is expected to be faster and more efficient than 4G.

Global Data Infrastructure and Cloud Services

Data today is the nerve centre of every organisation. The growing importance of data analytics — analysis of Big data flowing from ubiquitously networked end-user devices and IoT – has added to the value and growth of data centres.

Most organisations are investing in developing a data management infrastructure to collect data on production, sales, after-sales service, customer preferences, and so forth. There is a significant dependence on Big data for insights, real-time decision making and for optimising business performance; Such benefits has led to the establishment of data centres; Further IoT Edge, by connecting computing devices, will help to process and store this data using technologies like network-based cloud computing. To store data, companies are opting for exclusive (private cloud) data service or rented on-demand cloud from cloud service providers. Cloud services mark a paradigm shift in ICT provisioning, by allowing businesses and individuals to access on-demand IT services over a network, without the need to make huge investments in physical ICT infrastructure.

Conclusion

AI-powered interfaces, IoT, process automation, data analytics, etc. that were digital technology trends for the future until a few years ago have now become the expected norms of way of work and life in this decade, essentially, the thing of the day.

Business trends[4]

In the past decade, Cloud, Big data and IoT have remodelled IT operations, business models, and markets. The evolving dimensions of these technologies are resulting in the development of variant technologies such as blockchain, cognitive technologies, and digital reality that have become the leading disrupters in the digital arena.

---

4. *Tech Trends 2019: Beyond the Digital Frontier*, Deloitte Insights, 10th Anniversary Edition, (Deloitte Report, 2019) available at https://www2.deloitte.com/content/dam/Deloitte/fi/Documents/technology/DI_TechTrends2019.pdf.

Today, each of these technologies is poised to become a distinct macro force in its own right and will be the unifying underpinning for not only enterprise information technology (IT) but also corporate strategy. Immersive technologies like virtual reality (VR), augmented reality (AR), and mixed reality are increasingly being used by human in their interactions with their surroundings, with data and with each other. For example, in the 'new normal', retailers are creating VR and/or AR apps to help prospective customers visualise how an apparel or piece of jewellery will look like on them before they purchase it. Cognitive technologies like AI, ML, robotic process automation, natural language processing, and neural nets have demonstrated the ability to bring dramatic changes in business and society. The business of technology, digital transformation, and cyber, until recently trends, are now a vital aspect in doing business.

The OECD 2019 Report has called out these trends as the macro technology forces and one of the most pressing challenges that technology and business leaders will confront will be to extract and harness the value of these macro forces to deliver business results collectively.

In fact, the Deloitte Report[5] states that the factory of the future needs to bring together next-gen ERP, machine learning, embedded sensors across the production floor, augmented reality training, mobile visualisation and predictive flow scheduling, secure networks, and cloud-based tools for managing workflow across the supply chain; not to mention the need to retool workers and bring convergence of information technology and operational technology (IT/OT) roles and skills.[6]

The Deloitte Report specifies that these macro forces are enduring technology trends that will continue to shape strategies and dominate investment priorities. It further emphasised that these forces are not independent, isolated entities, rather they are partially compelling as standalone concerns; and one will have to decide what combination works for any given line of business, function, agency, or country to confidently chart a path beyond convention and organisational inertia; and to elevate the synergy moving beyond trends and beyond the digital frontier.[7]

5. *Ibid.*
6. Deloitte Report, 2019, pp 5-6.
7. Deloitte Report, 2019, p. 15.

AI-fuelled Organisations

The Deloitte Report states that AI's role in enterprises is growing as cognitive tools and tactics are standardised across IT environments. AI will be deployed not only to augment human performance but also to automate and reimagine operational and business processes. The upcoming times pave the way to fundamentally rethink the way humans and machines interact within working environments and what they can achieve together.[8]

Deloitte Report predicts in the next few years, among companies adopting AI technology, 70% will obtain AI capabilities through cloud-based enterprise software and 65% will create AI applications using cloud-based development services. Besides, data issues have been identified as among the top three greatest challenges faced with AI initiatives, states a Deloitte survey. As organisations move into the AI-fuelled model, workers will have to adapt to the more advanced ways of human-machine interactions and collaboration that until recently existed only in the realm of science fiction.[9]

Cloud/Serverless Computing

To save huge costs involved in operating and maintaining servers and to gain operational flexibility and other benefits, organisations are increasingly moving towards serverless computing, a spectrum of cloud-based options available to organisations[10].

The diagram depicts a cloud computing setup at work.

8. Deloitte Report, 2019, p. 34.
9. Deloitte Report, 2019, pp 23-25.
10. Deloitte Report, 2019, p. 40.

FIGURE 1

The digitalization of IT

Source: Deloitte analysis.

Source: Tech Trends 2019: Beyond Digital Frontier, Deloitte Report, 2019

The trend to move from setting up and maintaining internal servers to cloud/serverless computing, storage and memory[11] is gaining traction. Organisations having cloud-based models have redeployed their human resources to focus on their core business, nurture skills and learn new things. Thus, companies are increasingly focusing on process automation and transformation as part of their digital transformation initiatives.

11. Deloitte Report, 2019, p. 53.

Advanced Connectivity

There is a growing need to transmit the business data in real-time from where it is generated to where it is needed with the rapid development of networked devices. It involves decision on the formats of dissemination and, more importantly, on handling privacy issues. Given the scenario, businesses are looking for secure and advanced connectivity to transmit data efficiently, while also ensuring that privacy and other challenges associated with it are addressed simultaneously. Technology and business leaders anticipate that building blocks such as 5G, satellites, software defined networking, and network function visualisation can deliver an order-of-magnitude boost in network flexibility, efficiency, and velocity.[12]

Intelligent Interfaces

From traditional keyboards and keypads to touchscreens (smartphones), intelligent interfaces are moving towards voice commands to make the device work without having to touch it. This works in combination with other technologies such as computer vision, conversational voice, auditory analytics, and advanced AR and VR. These capabilities will also change the way humans engage with machines, data, and each other.[13]

Experience Marketing

In beyond marketing or experience marketing, the customer is the centre stage of all business decisions. Increasingly, companies are trying to understand individual customer's preferences and behaviours. Tailored content, along with identification and adoption of the best delivery method across physical and digital touchpoints, is making individual customer journeys unique. This approach calls for the strategic deployment of a new set of tools and tactics that will help companies elevate their marketing operations from art to a blend of art and science, while keeping the customer firmly at the centre of all its decisions.

Tools and Technologies Addressing Cyber and Other Risks

From managing cyber and privacy risks as discrete functions, usually happening in the last stage of the product life cycle, organisations have now felt the need to integrate this throughout the product life cycle, making cyber

12. Deloitte Report, 2019, p. 67.
13. Deloitte Report, 2019, p. 71.

and other risks as a shared responsibility of all those connected to the product life cycle. Engaging people throughout the product development process ensures that these potential risks are addressed proactively in a timely and efficient manner. This has become a prerequisite as quality of the product or service is the key to its success.

Business Models

The digital economy has given rise to new business models, which are discussed in the OECD Report on Action 1: Addressing the tax challenges of the digital economy. The most popular business model is the online retailer model in which the transaction of sale happens on online platforms (these platforms connect buyers and sellers) in return for a transaction or placement fee or a commission. Examples of such businesses include Amazon, Flipkart, and Alibaba. Social media is another model, mainly deriving revenue from the advertisements placed on its platforms. Some examples of this include Facebook, Xing, and Qzone. In the subscription model, platforms like Netflix and Spotify render services by charging a subscription fee for continued access to digital content (e.g., music or videos). Finally, the collaborative platform model enables sharing of 'access' to resources rather than owning them outright. Platforms charge a fixed or variable fee for use of resources. Examples of such businesses include Airbnb, BlaBlaCar, and Didi Chuxing.

OECD classifies new business models under the digital economy as follows:

- Business to Business model
- Business to Consumer model
- Consumer to Consumer model

The OECD, in its interim report[14], discusses the emergence of new business models in the digital economy. Businesses interact with users through different types of online or web-based interfaces. The multi-sided platform contains indirect network externalities, affecting the price structures across market sides. Additionally, the platform allows direct interactions between

14. OECD/G20 Base Erosion and Profit Shifting Project *Tax Challenges Arising from Digitalisation – Interim Report, 2018* (OECD Interim Report, 2018).

end-users on different market sides, and end-users on each market side have to affiliate themselves with the platform (implying non-zero switching costs). For the classification to be effective, it is important to specify that it categorises business models or, differently said, business lines and not overall companies.

A brief summary of the additional business models is stated below.

> "**Multi-sided platforms:** These platforms allow end-users to exchange and transact with participant groups, while leaving control rights and liabilities towards customers mostly with the supplier; end-users affiliate with the platform and interact across market sides so that indirect networks become crucial, e.g., Uber, Didi Chuxing, Airbnb, Xiaozhu, BlaBlaCar, Weibo, Amazon Marketplace, Taobao, Facebook, NetEase, or Google, Deliveroo, Foodora, and UberEATS.
>
> **Resellers:** Businesses that acquire products, including control rights, from suppliers and resell them to buyers; resellers control prices and assume liability towards customers; they do not allow interaction with end-users, and they do not necessarily require customers to affiliate to the online platform, e.g., Amazon e-commerce, Alibaba, JD.com, Spotify, Tencent's music distribution, or Netflix (where it purchases content).
>
> **Vertically integrated firms:** Businesses that have acquired ownership over suppliers and have, thus, integrated the supply side of the market within their business, e.g., Amazon e-commerce (warehousing and logistics), Xiaomi (end user devices and applications), Huawei (hardware and cloud computing), and Netflix (film production).
>
> **Input suppliers:** Businesses or individuals supplying intermediary inputs required for the production of goods or services in another firm. In contrast to multi-sided platforms, input suppliers are not intermediaries and interact only with the other firm and not with the final customer (e.g., Intel or Tsinghua Unigroup)."[15]

The distinguishing features of digitised business models set them apart from traditional businesses.

- **Cross-jurisdictional scale without mass:** This challenges the traditional way of doing business in any jurisdiction by having a

15. OECD Interim Report, 2018, pp 30-31.

physical (brick and mortar) presence. Any stage of the business process can be facilitated from any jurisdiction due to digitalisation which allows organisations to participate in cross-jurisdictional sale or operations without mass.[16]

- **Reliance on intangible assets, including intellectual property:** Digitalised businesses invest heavily in intangibles, especially assets like software, websites, and algorithms, which are vital for their value chain and operation, and can either be owned or leased from a third party.
- **Data, user participation and their synergies with IP:** Business models of highly digitalised companies include data, user participation, network effects and the provision of user-generated content. The benefits of data analysis increase with the amount of information collected.
- **Switching cost and lock-in effect:** Digital transactions can be carried out on different electronic devices, though end-users often rely on different operating systems, resulting in a lock-in to a particular operating system.
- **Complimentary nature:** Customers derive more benefits by consuming two (or more) complimentary goods or services.
- **Direct network effects:** The utility from consumption of specific goods or services is often dependent on the number of end-users consuming them.
- **Indirect network effects:** In certain digital business models, a specific group of end-users benefit from interacting with another group of end-users via an online platform.
- **Negligible marginal cost:** Production of digital goods and services often entails higher fixed costs and lower variable costs.
- **Relationship between digitalised business models and value creation:** User participation (reviews, ratings, provision of services) builds trust and reputation, contributes to brand value, and growth of user networks and utility beyond the consumption of service.

16. OECD Interim Report, 2018, p. 51.

The concept of value creation has evolved significantly in the digital economy. Traditionally, value chain is defined as converting inputs into outputs through discrete but, maybe, related sequential activities. The value chain concept has been popularised and commonly analysed by American academic and writer Michael E. Porter. The traditional value creation theory comprises five primary activities - inbound and outbound logistics, marketing & sales, and servcies; and four support activities - infrastructure, human resoruce management, technology development, and procurement.

The emerging models of value creation in the digital world vary from the traditional theory. These models are stated below:

- **Value networks:** Value is created through activities performed in a concurrent manner, relying on mediating technology. This is a common framework for many highly digitalised companies which rely on a mediating technology that is used by platform operators to link customers interested in engaging in a transaction or relationship. A ride-for-hire company and a social network are prominent examples of value networks.
- **Value shops:** These are cyclical value systems characterised by intensive use of customised technology to solve a specific customer demand/problem. These operate on single-sided markets where interactions take place with one specific type of user or customer. A cloud computing company is an example of this model.

Blockchain

A blockchain is a software mechanism that enables distributed ledger technology. It allows recording and tracking of transactions and resources without the presence of a centralised or regulatory authority. Every transaction needs to be validated before it is executed and the validation occurs in a cryptographic manner. These validations are carried out by miners. The name 'blockchain' is suggestive of the way the mechanism of 'blockchain' works, as it is a series of data blocks each containing information typically relating to four aspects: a reference to previous block, list of included transactions (including its summary), a time stamp, and proof that ensures the nodes stay true which is optional. These blocks then form a chain, leaving an unalterable trail. This ensures transparency.

Blockchains are of various types. In a 'public blockchain', the transactions occur between the interested sections of the public, e.g., 'bitcoin'. A 'private blockchain', on the other hand, is a controlled blockchain where access rights are given only to authorised persons, e.g., blockchain adopted by a business organisation for its internal functions. A hybrid model of public and private blockchain is termed as 'consortium blockchain', and its use is driven by the necessity to incorporate both public and private blockchain features. In the hybrid model, users require permission rights to access the blockchain which works like a public blockchain.

Various countries and organisations, particularly businesses, are extensively exploring the application of blockchain technology in the fields of crypto-currencies, contracts, financial services, gaming, supply chain networks, among others.

Bitcoins

Bitcoin, a popular cryptocurrency, is based on the blockchain technology. Believed to have been developed by Satoshi Nakamoto of Japan, bitcoin works like a payment app where a bitcoin wallet is downloaded by the user to make payments for online transactions. Traditional currency can be used to buy bitcoins,[17] and bitcoins can be encashed into traditional currency at various bitcoin exchanges. As the price of bitcoins depends on the demand-supply equation or, in some cases, pre-determined by the bitcoin exchanges, the price difference tends to create arbitrage opportunities.

India does not recognise bitcoin as a legal currency and, presently, there is no regulation to deal with this digital asset. Given this scenario, users fear trading in bitcoins and the government is apprehensive about the use of bitcoins for illegal activities. Several countries do not recognise the bitcoin as legal tender. Countries like Argentina and Russia restrict/ban currencies, while in countries like Thailand's limited licensing policy restricts the operations of entities such as Bitcoin exchanges.

Nonetheless, countries worldwide are now working towards bringing in legislation to deal with cryptocurrency, specifically due to the integration of this new technology with the existing regulated financial system. The

17. The indicative value of one Bitcoin in INR terms was USD 5379.7 on April 27, 2019 (URL:https://www.tradingview.com/markets/cryptocurrencies/prices-bitcoin/).

Financial Crimes Enforcement Network (FinCEN), a bureau in the United States Treasury Department, has issued a non-binding guidance on characterisation rules for certain activities involving virtual currencies.

Chapter 2

TAXATION ASPECTS OF THE DIGITAL ECONOMY

International Taxation

The integration of national economies and markets has increased substantially in recent years, putting a strain on international tax rules which were formulated more than a century ago. Digital technology has revolutionised the way businesses operate in the current world, where companies can sell their services and goods in new markets from remote locations without being physically present in the client's jurisdiction. This leads to a unique problem of mismatch between the places where profits are created (customers' jurisdictions) and where the earnings and profits are taxed (the jurisdiction/location where the company is officially registered/established). International tax practices formulated for the traditional brick-and-mortar economy fail to address the tax challenges of the modern digital economy. Thus, the digital economy is more vulnerable to taxation from the international tax perspective.

The digital economy poses several challenges right from the issue of evaluating a transaction's characterisation, to determining its nexus, to identifying the taxing rights of the countries, to ascertaining how the transaction eventually needs to be taxed. One of the key issues is the difficulty to identify and attribute costs and returns with the Organisation for Economic Co-operation and Development (OECD) defined Development, Enhancement, Maintenance, Protection and Exploitation (DEMPE) life cycle of intellectual property and other intangible assets.

Besides, the ability of digital enterprises is to avoid taxes by artificially segregating the taxable income from the activities that generate it, or in the case of value-added tax (VAT), paying no or an inappropriately low amount of tax on remote digital supplies in order to exempt businesses or multi-location enterprises (MLEs).

Certain taxpayers resort to measures like shifting taxable income from the jurisdiction in which the income-producing activities are conducted, resulting in 'base erosion and profit shifting' (BEPS)[18] activities. The instances include avoiding taxable presence, low or no withholding tax at source, and permanent establishment (PE) structures that generate little taxable profit vis-à-vis real activities undertaken by enterprises. In addition, rights in intangibles and returns can be transferred to an associated enterprise in whose jurisdiction the income earned from said intangibles is subject to low or no tax on account of preferential tax regime, etc. Weaknesses in the current rules create opportunities for BEPS which not only lead to a competitive disadvantage for domestic enterprises or for those that do not resort to BEPS but also undermines the integrity of the tax system and potentially increases the difficulty of reaching revenue goals.

BEPS Analysis

To address the BEPS concerns, the OECD released a 15-point action plan in 2015 which discusses the BEPS challenges and provided some recommendations like amending the domestic tax laws in line with its suggestions to ensure that the countries you do business with respect the bilateral tax treaty obligations.

The BEPS measures are designed on the principle that profits are to be taxed where economic activities take place and value is created. Action 1 of the BEPS project deals with tax challenges due to digitalisation.

In 2018, OECD released an interim report on the steps taken and progress made towards addressing the BEPS concerns/challenges of the digital economy. Although the OECD did not recommend specific interim measures, it rather set design principles. The members agreed to review the impact of digitalisation on nexus and profit allocation rules while working towards a final report in 2020 aimed at providing a consensus-based long-term solution.

18. Base Erosion Profit Sharing (BEPS) refers to tax planning strategies that exploit gaps and mismatches in tax rules to make profits 'disappear' for tax purposes or to shift profits to locations where there is little or no real activity; but the taxes are low, resulting in little or no overall corporate tax being paid.

Public Consultant Document

OECD in 2019 had sought public opinion on the possible solutions to the tax challenges posed by the digital economy and promised to analyse and incorporate constructive recommendations in its final report.

Response of Countries

The ensuing section summarises the actions taken by some countries that have selectively implemented OECD's recommendations in their domestic tax laws.

Equalisation Levy by India

India introduced equalisation levy from June 1, 2016, on consideration received or receivable for any specified services. The scope of equalisation levy has been widened by the Finance Act, 2020[19]. Presently, the only specified service notified is online advertisement, any provision for digital advertising space or any other facility or service for the purpose of online advertisement. However, the definition could be broadened in scope over a period of time.

Equalisation levy is payable on the amount of consideration received or receivable by a non-resident from (a) a person resident in India and carrying on business or profession, or (b) a non-resident having a permanent establishment in India. However, this is required to be deducted by the persons remitting the consideration in (a) and (b) above. The rate of levy is 6% of the amount of consideration for any specified services. Further, a threshold for exemption is provided where consideration received or receivable does not exceed ₹100,000.

Introduction of 'Significant Economic Presence' by India

India introduced the concept of 'significant economic presence' (SEP)[20] in its domestic tax law by deeming the significant economic presence of a non-resident to constitute 'business connection' in India.

19. For detailed discussion refer Chapter 3.
20. SEP introduced in the Income-Tax Act, 1961 from April 1, 2018.

Significant economic presence is defined to mean transactions for any goods, services or property carried out by a non-resident in India, including the provision of download of data or software in India, provided the revenue therefrom exceeds the prescribed monetary threshold; or the systematic and continuous soliciting of business activities or engaging in interaction with users (exceeding the number as may be prescribed) in India through digital means. Factors such as (a) whether the agreement for such transactions or activities is entered in India or not, or (b) whether the non-resident has a residence or place of business in India, or (c) whether the non-resident renders services in India, are not relevant. SEP stipulates the income threshold that is attributable to the specified transactions or activities to be deemed to accrue or arise in India.

The threshold of 'revenue' and 'users' will be decided by the government in consultation with the stakeholders. Cross border business profits, however, will continue to be taxed as per the existing treaty rules until India renegotiates the existing tax treaties for inclusion of the new nexus rule.

The Memorandum to the Finance Bill, 2018 included the following justification by Govt of India to bring SEP into existence under the provision of the Income-tax Act, 1961 ('the Act'):

> "For a long time, nexus based on physical presence was used as a proxy to regular economic allegiance of a non-resident. However, with the advancement in information and communication technology in the last few decades, new business models operating remotely through digital medium have emerged. Under these new business models, the non-resident enterprises interact with customers in another country without having any physical presence in that country resulting in avoidance of taxation in the source country. Therefore, the existing nexus rule based on physical presence do not hold good anymore for taxation of business profits in source country. As a result, the rights of the source country to tax business profits that are derived from its economy is unfairly and unreasonably eroded".

The intention of this SEP legislation was to bring to tax the non-residents who have been doing business with India through digital medium without paying the tax in India.

With this background, the Government of India has introduced the Explanation 2A to Section 9(i) w.e.f. 1st April 2019 (AY 2019-20) and subsequently it was deferred and made it applicable w.e.f. 1st April 2021 (Assessment Year 2022-23). SEP has been defined in the said explanation as under:

(a) Transaction in respect of any goods, services or property carried out by a non-resident in India, including the provision of download of data or software in India, subject to exceeding the threshold limit of aggregate payment to be prescribed; or

(b) Systematic and continuous soliciting of business activities or engaging in interaction with such number of users as may be prescribed, in India through digital means.

Amendments

In view of the above back ground, the CBDT *vide* its notification No.41/2021/F.No 370142/11/2018-TPL, dated 3 May 2021 prescribed the threshold limit for the purpose of clause (a) and (b) above as under:

(1) For the purposes of clause (a) of *Explanation 2A* to clause (i) of sub-section (1) of section 9, the amount of aggregate of payments arising from transaction or transactions in respect of any goods, services or property carried out by a non-resident with any person in India, including provision of download of data or software in India during the previous year, shall be **two crore rupees**;

(2) For the purposes of clause (b) of *Explanation 2A* to clause (i) of sub-section (1) of section 9, the number of users with whom systematic and continuous business activities are solicited or who are engaged in interaction shall be **three lakhs**.

Impact of the Amendments

The above legislation and the subsequent notification have created difficulties in implementation on the part of the taxpayer and may cause significant burden of compliance on the Indian consumers buying the goods or availing the services.

The reading of the present provisions of SEP gives the impression that these provisions are applicable to all companies including the import of goods to India in physical form or under traditional method. Consequent to the applicability of SEP provisions, the Non-resident Seller is deemed to have business connection in India upon crossing the threshold limit prescribed and therefore, the income from such transactions is deemed to accrue or arise in India and accordingly, liable to pay tax in India under the provisions of the Act.

However, it may be noted that section 90 of the Act provides an option to a non-resident to be taxed either under the provisions of the Act or Tax Treaty of the country of its residence, whichever is most beneficial to him.

In effect, the tax liability on such transactions would be nullified by applying the narrow definition provided under the provisions of Article 5 – "Permanent establishment" and Article 7 – "Business Profits" of Tax Treaty between India and the respective country of residence unless the Tax Treaty is amendment by the Government, whereby the non-resident is not liable to pay tax in India if he does not have any permanent establishment in India.

In order to access the afore stated Tax Treaty benefit, the non-resident is required to furnish following documents:

(a) Tax Residency certificate

(b) Form No.10F

(c) No-PE declaration (stating that he does not have a PE in India)

If it is held as applicable to physical imports, it is not the intention of the law as the law seeks to tax income arising out of E-commerce. Further assuming it is held as applicable, the number of imports is quite high in any organisation making it very onerous to comply with this provision of law.

With respect to imports from Non Tax Treaty Countries, Indian Companies making payments to non-residents would not be able to determine the revenue/profit attributable to India, so they may have to apply 40% (plus applicable surcharge and cess) on the gross payments in the absence of specific guidelines in this regard or request the non-resident to get a lower withholding tax order from the tax department in India for the transactions carried out in India.

Further, since the import transactions with third parties are always at arm's length and the transactions with associated enterprises are subject to transfer pricing provisions, there exists seldom any scope for income escapement from tax.

Upon application of SEP provisions, Indian importers of goods in physical form or under traditional method are required to make an assessment of applicability of withholding tax provisions on the income deemed to accrue or arise to Non-resident Seller in India in each case and this makes the compliance onerous on the part of Indian importers for the reasons mentioned above, but the end result would be nothing unless the Tax Treaties are amended by the Government.

What Government Should Do

The Government should clarify immediately on the following lines:

- The Government of India should clarify that these provisions are applicable only for Digital Commerce or E Commerce transactions and not all imports.
- The reading of this provisions also leads to an interpretation that if any Indian importer is accessing their internal computer system for placing order for goods it may lead to SEP provisions and again it is not intended.
- Hence the government should clarify that these provisions are applicable only for companies carrying business of E Commerce or business of digital Economy.
- The Government of India/CBDT should clarify that keeping in mind the object of introduction of SEP provisions it should exclude/exempt the physical form/traditional method of imports from the SEP provisions and provide relief to the Indian importer of goods under the physical form/traditional method from the compliance of withholding tax provisions.
- The threshold of Rs. 2 Crore per annum prescribed for Non-resident selling goods to the customers present whole of India is too less and consequently it becomes applicable for each and every transaction, hence the threshold exemption loses its significance. Therefore, the

Government of India should increase the threshold limit to Rs. 200 Crore per annum (instead of Rs. 2 Crore).

- Further if the physical form of goods is considered as part of SEP, it should be clarified that section 90(2) of Income-tax Act is applicable and if the Foreign Company has no PE the income is not taxable and no consequential provisions to be applied.

Digital Economy and Permanent Establishment

Typically, a tax treaty provides resident-based taxation of business profits. However, if the profits arise through a permanent establishment (PE) in the Source state, then the Source state gets the right to tax such business profits but only to the extent of profits attributable to the PE.

Under the PE concept, a Source state justifies taxation by measuring the level of economic presence of a foreign enterprise in the state. An objective criterion, largely based on the traditional requirement of 'physical presence' in the Source state, is used for the purpose. The PE definition initially comprised two distinct thresholds: (i) a fixed place through which the business of the enterprise is wholly or partly carried on, or where no place of business can be found, (ii) a person acting on behalf of the foreign enterprise and habitually exercising authority to conclude contracts on behalf of the foreign enterprise. In both situations, a certain level of physical presence in the source jurisdiction is required, either directly or through an agent. An additional threshold based on the performance of services by employees (or other persons receiving instructions) of a non-resident enterprise was also included thereafter, and this is applicable irrespective of whether the services are performed through a fixed place of business or not. However, under it, certain activity-specific exemptions are available (such as maintaining a warehouse/storage, display facility, processing, etc.). These do not constitute a PE.

In many digital economy business models, a non-resident company may interact with customers in a foreign country through a website or other digital means (e.g., through an app on a mobile device) without maintaining a physical presence in the country. Increasing reliance on automated processes may further decrease reliance on local or physical presence.

While the ability of companies to maintain some level of business connection within a country without being subject to tax on business profits —earned from sources within that country — is not unique to digital businesses, it is available at a greater scale in the digital economy. In the web economy, this ability, coupled with strategies that eliminate taxation in the state of residence, often results in such revenue not being taxed anywhere, thereby raising BEPS concerns.

Moreover, under certain circumstances, tax in a Source state can be ingeniously avoided by fragmenting operations among multiple group entities in order to qualify for exceptions to PE status for preparatory and auxiliary activities, or by ensuring that each location through which business is conducted falls below the PE threshold. Further, activities that previously may have been preparatory or auxiliary may have now become key components of an enterprise's business. Arrangements of these types give rise to BEPS concerns.

In view of the aforesaid, there is an immediate need to alter the rules and create alternate thresholds for digital enterprises from the PE perspective. The OECD in its Action Report 1 stated that the above concerns need to be tackled as one of the major action points and the discussion in this regard is summarised below.

Altering Rules Regarding Specific Activity Exemptions

It was agreed to modify the list of exceptions in the PE definition to ensure that each of the exceptions included therein is restricted to activities of a 'preparatory or auxiliary' character, and to introduce an anti-fragmentation rule so that companies do not take advantage of the fragmentation exception by conducting business activities among closely related enterprises.

For example, an online seller's large local warehouse — with a significant workforce to store and deliver goods sold online to customers — would now constitute the seller's permanent establishment under the new standard, as his or her business model relies on the warehouse for proximity and quick delivery to customers. These changes to the definition of PE of the OECD Model Tax Convention are included in the Action 7 Report – Preventing the Artificial Avoidance of PE Status (OECD, 2015)[21]. They are now expected to

21. OECD (2015), *Preventing the Artificial Avoidance of Permanent Establishment Status*, Action 7 - 2015 Final Report, OECD/G20 Base Erosion and Profit Shifting Project, OECD Publishing, Paris, https://doi.org/10.1787/9789264241220-en; last accessed on July 08, 2021.

be implemented across the existing tax treaty network in a synchronised and efficient manner by concluding the multilateral instrument that modifies bilateral tax treaties under Action 15.

Altering Rules Relating to Agency PE

It was also agreed to modify the definition of PE to address circumstances in which artificial arrangements relating to the sales of goods or services of one company by a sister company of a multinational enterprise (MNE) is effectively construed as the conclusion of sales contract by the sister concern and not the original company.

For example, where the sales force of a local subsidiary of an online seller of tangible products or an online provider of advertising services habitually plays the principal role in concluding contracts with clients for the parent company's products or services, and these contracts are routinely concluded without material modification by the parent company; then, this activity would result in a permanent establishment for the parent company. This is also expected to be implemented across the existing tax treaty network through the conclusion of the multilateral instrument.

New Digital Nexus Based PE – Significant Economic Presence

A non-resident enterprise that shows evidence of a purposeful and sustained interaction with the economy of a foreign country through technology or other automated tools will now create a taxable presence in that country under the digital nexus-based PE — significant economic presence. These factors will be combined with the revenue derived from remote transactions, to ensure that only cases of significant economic presence are covered, thereby minimising compliance costs of the taxpayers and providing certainty for cross-border activities.

Revenue based factors, user-based factors and digital factors have been discussed by the OECD in its report on Action 1. Although the OECD has not provided any recommendations, it has stated that countries could introduce any of these three options in their domestic laws or in their bilateral tax treaties, as additional safeguards against BEPS, as long as the provisions respect existing treaty obligations.

Some countries have adopted these options by making amendments or new interpretations of the PE threshold in their domestic tax laws. These are generally aimed at diluting the requirement for permanence and physical presence at a specific geographical location to establish a nexus for net-basis taxation. These measures generally deem a PE to exist in circumstances where one would not ordinarily exist if the traditional PE definition were applied.

India, through the Finance Act, 2018, has amended its domestic tax law and provided for the significant economic presence approach.

Conclusion

Most countries have adopted or are in the process of adopting unilateral actions, as an interim measure, to tackle the digital economy challenges, even as they wait for the OECD Report to provide a consensus-based resolution to taxing the digital economy ecosystem. A detailed summary of each country and their action steps on proposals on Direct Taxes is given in Annexure 1.

Transfer Pricing and Attribution of Profits

Treaty rules on business profits stipulate that only profits 'attributable' to the PE are taxable in the jurisdiction where the PE is located. These are profits that the PE would be expected to make if it were a distinct and separate enterprise.

In its public consultation document, issued on February 13, 2019, OECD has put forth proposals for resolving tax challenges of the existing profit allocation and nexus rules through the following proposals that are currently being discussed in various jurisdictions.

(i) **User participation proposal:** This approach focuses on businesses where significant value is created through digital presence and user participation. In certain highly digitalised businesses, value is created through developing an active user base and soliciting data and content contributions from those users. The activities and participation of users contributes to increasing brand value, generating valuable data and to developing a critical mass of users that help to establish market power. Digitised businesses like social media platforms, search engines, and online marketplaces are key examples.

In such cases, the OECD suggests that profit ought to be allocated to the relevant jurisdictions regardless of whether the business has a local/physical presence in the user jurisdiction. The attributable profit for the user jurisdiction due to user participation would be calculated through a non-routine or residual profit-split approach, and not by applying the traditional arm's length principle. A proportion of the residual non-routine profits would be attributed to the value created by user activities and allocated to the countries in which the users reside. The calculation will be based using an agreed allocation metric, while profits attributable to routine activities would continue to be determined according to current rules.

The Consultation document acknowledges the practical challenges in calculating non-routine profit, particularly at the level of an individual business line. A pragmatic approach, using formulae to approximate value combined with strong dispute resolution mechanisms could help avoid disputes between countries.

(ii) **Marketing intangibles proposal:** This approach identifies valuable marketing intangibles[22] (for all taxpayers) and assigns some or all of the returns on those intangibles to the market jurisdictions. The 'marketing intangibles' proposal is envisaged for a scenario where an MNE penetrates a jurisdiction, either remotely or through a limited local presence (such as Limited Risk Distributor), to develop a user/customer base and other marketing intangibles. An intrinsic functional link exists between marketing intangibles and the market jurisdiction. Marketing intangibles could consist of the positive value that customers have towards a brand (brand image), or even customer data that could provide valuable insights on the customer base in a market jurisdiction.

There are three key fact patterns under which non-routine profit attributable to the use of marketing intangibles would be allocated and taxed in the market jurisdiction:

22. Marketing intangibles would have the same meaning as set forth in the OECD Transfer Pricing Guidelines, 2017. OECD (2017), *OECD Transfer Pricing Guidelines for Multinational Enterprises and Tax Administrations 2017,* OECD Publishing, Paris, https://doi.org/10.1787/tpg-2017-en; last accessed on July 8, 2021.

- A highly digitalised business deriving revenues from sales and marketing activities targeting a market jurisdiction in which it does not have a taxable presence;
- A highly digitalised business with a local presence that operates as a limited risk distributor; and
- A consumer product business that is not highly digitalised, but operates either remotely with no physical presence or through a limited risk distributor.

According to the consultation document, the user participation proposal and the marketing intangible proposal would both reach a broadly similar tax outcome under the first two fact patterns.

Contrary to the existing profit allocation and nexus rules, under this proposal, tax authorities of the market jurisdiction would be entitled to tax some or all of the non-routine income associated with such marketing intangibles and their attendant risks. The allocation of non-routine returns from marketing intangibles would apply irrespective of the legal title of the marketing intangible, DEMPE functions related to the intangibles, or how risks related to marketing intangibles would be allocated under the existing transfer pricing rules. The allocation of profits attributable to technology-related intangibles generated by R&D or attributable to routine functions would be unchanged.

The non-routine or residual profits generated by the marketing intangibles could be determined through either (i) normal transactional transfer pricing principles dependent on the economic contribution to profits provided by the marketing intangibles, or (ii) a revised profit split analysis, potentially using mechanical approaches.

The proposal excludes trade intangibles which, as per the OECD, do not possess similar intrinsic functional link with market jurisdictions. The proposal if implemented would be applicable to all businesses and not just digital businesses. The OECD envisages that this proposal would modify current transfer pricing and treaty rules and require marketing intangibles and risks associated with such intangibles to be allocated to the market jurisdiction.

(iii) **Significant economic presence proposal:** This approach propounds that a taxable presence would arise in a jurisdiction when a non-resident enterprise has a significant economic presence in a market jurisdiction through purposeful and sustained interaction with customers through digital technology and other automated means. Digitalisation of the economy and other technological advances have enabled business enterprises to be heavily involved in the economic life of a jurisdiction without a significant physical presence which has effectively rendered the existing nexus and profit allocation rules ineffective.

In order to trigger a taxable presence, an entity would be required to earn revenues on a sustained basis along with other factors that could include the existence of a user base and associated data; the volume of digital content derived from the jurisdiction; billing and collection in local currency or with local form of payment; maintenance of a website in a local language; responsibility for the final delivery of goods to customers or other support services (e.g. after-sales service, repairs and maintenance); or sustained marketing and sales promotion activities (whether online or not) to attract customers. The revenue-generating activity of the non-resident enterprise would need to be linked to its significant economic presence.

Profit allocation mechanism in a significant economic presence could be based on a number of mechanisms like the fractional apportionment method in which the tax base would be determined by applying the global profit rate of the group to the revenues generated in a jurisdiction and then apportioning the tax base using an agreed weighting of allocation keys such as sales, assets and employees. Consideration would be given to the use of a withholding tax as a collection mechanism and enforcement tool.

Although the BEPS package has made significant progress in aligning taxation with value creation and has managed to curtail double non-taxation, there is still a perceived risk of profit shifting to low/no tax jurisdictions by a number of jurisdictions. This risk is particularly acute in connection with profits relating to intangibles, prevalent in the digital economy, as well as in a broader context. For instance, group entities that are financed with equity capital and generate profits from intra-group financing or similar activities and subject to no or low taxes in the jurisdictions where those entities are established. In light of the above, the OECD has suggested 'the global anti-base erosion proposal'. This proposal contemplates the possible imposition of a withholding tax as a collection mechanism and enforcement tool. In this context, consideration could be given to a gross-basis withholding tax at a low rate on payments to an enterprise with a significant economic presence, with the enterprise having the right to file an income tax return and seek a refund if the withheld amount exceeded the enterprise's income tax liability. Although the OECD does not indicate any specific business to which this approach would apply, any business that penetrates into market jurisdictions with sustained digital intervention and negligible physical presence would fall under this umbrella. The OECD has put forth a two-part proposal of two inter-related rules: (i) an income inclusion rule and (ii) a tax on base eroding payments.

(i) **Income inclusion rule:** A shareholder with a significant (e.g., 25%) ownership interest in a corporation would be required to bring into account a proportionate share of the income of that corporation if that income was not subject to tax above a minimum rate. The rule would be applied on a country-by-country basis, with credit available on the same basis for any underlying tax paid. This would ensure that the income of the MNE is subject to tax at a minimum rate, thereby reducing the incentive to allocate returns for tax reasons to low taxed entities. The rule would build on Action Plan No. 3 recommendations and would draw on aspects of the US regime for taxing global intangible low-taxed income (GILTI).

    The amount of income to be included would be calculated under domestic rules and shareholders would be entitled to claim a credit for any underlying tax paid on the attributed income, with such credits also being calculated on a jurisdiction-by-jurisdiction basis.

(ii) **Tax on base-eroding payments:** The second key element of the proposal is a tax on base eroding payments that complements the income inclusion rule by allowing a source jurisdiction to protect itself from the risk of base eroding payments. The proposal would involve:

- An 'undertaxed payments rule' that would deny a deduction for certain defined categories of payment to a related party or payment unless those payments were subject to a minimum effective rate of tax. A related party could be based on a 25% common ownership test.

- A complementary 'subject-to-tax rule' would be incorporated into double tax treaties that would grant certain treaty benefits only if the item of income is sufficiently taxed in the other state. This proposal is designed to complement the income inclusion rule by allowing a source jurisdiction to tax what it considers to be base-eroding payments.

The existing BEPS rule and the current consultation paper intend to address the same problem of base erosion of profit, and hence it is likely that there could be an overlap with existing rules. Given the potential for overlap, an ordering rule would be required with clear instructions on the implementation. While the consultation paper is yet to assume finality, the paper puts forth innovative approaches to tackle the problem of taxation of value creation under a digital economy which is a significant departure from the existing global tax architecture.

Taxation of Bitcoins

Bitcoin taxation is specifically not dealt within the domestic tax laws of many countries including India. It could typically fall in one of the categories: capital gains or business income or residual income. Another aspect, however, that investor group push relates to treatment of bitcoins as currency and any differences arising therefrom, consequentially, to be treated as currency fluctuations.

The US Government has issued a notice stating that virtual currency be treated as 'property' for US federal tax purposes. The UK Government has released a guidance paper[23] which provides an overview of tax treatment for transactions involving cryptocurrencies, specifically bitcoins. It discusses the issue of characterizing income arising from such transactions and provides when such income would be considered as business income or capital gains or other category. The South African Government's stance reveals that it considers cryptocurrencies as assets of an intangible nature. Other countries are also likely to share their views on how to treat and tax bitcoins.

23. https://assets.publishing.service.gov.uk/government/uploads/system/uploads/attachment_data/file/752070/cryptoassets_taskforce_final_report_final_web.pdf.

In this context, it is worthwhile to discuss the first judicial decision of the Israeli District Court, pronounced on May 19, 2019, on taxation of bitcoin transactions by individuals. The taxpayer considered the profit as currency fluctuation other than in the course of a business, which is exempt from tax in Israel. The court ruled that bitcoin is neither currency nor foreign currency, but rather it falls within the definition of an asset in accordance with the circular issued by the Israeli Government on the matter. The District Court therefore ruled that profits generated from the sale of bitcoins should be subject to capital gains tax.

Supreme Court Ruling on Bitcoins in *Internet and Mobile Association of India v. Reserve Bank of India*[24]

The use of cryptocurrency is a contentious issue, with its legality being a mystery to the public. Bitcoins are a form of digital currency and are not considered to be legal tender. However, they can function as a medium of exchange akin to money. The lack of a traditional government or bank-backed system to regulate its use makes cryptocurrencies the target of several concerns such as it being a conduit for black money or anonymously funding terrorism. Despite the odds, cryptocurrencies have gained popularity worldwide and the cryptocurrency market in India has also been slowly gathering momentum.

Reserve Bank of India (RBI) issued a **"Statement on Developmental and Regulatory Policies"**[25] on April 5, 2018, paragraph 13 of which directed the entities regulated by RBI (i) not to deal with or provide services to any individual or business entities dealing with or settling virtual currencies (VCs), and (ii) to exit the relationship, if they already have one, with such individuals/business entities, dealing with or settling VCs.

Following the said statement, RBI also issued a circular[26] dated April 6, 2018, in exercise of the powers conferred by section 35A read with section 36(1)(a) ; section 56 of the Banking Regulation Act, 1949; section 45JA

24. 2020 SCC Online SC 275.
25. Available at https://www.rbi.org.in/Scripts/BS_PressReleaseDisplay.aspx?prid=51078#:~:text=This%20Statement%20sets%20out%20various,and%20(v)%20consumer%20protection; last accessed on July 08, 2021.
26. Available at https://rbi.org.in/Scripts/BS_CircularIndexDisplay.aspx?Id=11243; last accessed on July 08, 2021.

and section 45L of the Reserve Bank of India Act, 1934 (hereinafter 'RBI Act, 1934') and section 10(2) read with section 18 of the Payment and Settlement Systems Act, 2007, directing the entities regulated by RBI

(i) not to deal in VCs nor to provide services for facilitating any person or entity in dealing with or settling virtual currencies, and

(ii) to exit the relationship with such persons or entities, if they were already providing such services to them.

The said statement and circular were challenged before the Supreme Court. In its decision,[27] the Supreme Court, upon analysing the validity of the cryptocurrency circular, concluded it to be incorrect and was struck down.

A three-judge bench held the circular to be a disproportionate regulatory action in a decision that suggests cryptocurrencies should be subject to considered regulation and not blanket prohibition, under Indian law.

Key Arguments before Supreme Court against the Circular

- The RBI has no jurisdiction to act in this manner, as cryptocurrencies are neither 'currency' nor a 'payment system', which are regulated by the RBI. Merely because cryptocurrencies can be used in a manner akin to money does not change the essential legal characteristic of cryptocurrencies, which resemble tradable digital goods or commodities more than they resemble a form of currency, and are thus outside the RBI's usual scope of regulation.
- The circular amounted to an arbitrary, unfair, and unconstitutional restriction on a legitimate business activity. In the absence of a 'legislative' ban on cryptocurrencies that declares them *res extra commercium*, the use of, and trade in, cryptocurrencies is a legitimate business activity.
- The circular effectively placed a complete ban on the use of cryptocurrencies, and such a ban was unreasonable, disproportionate, and based on an erroneous understanding that it was impossible to regulate cryptocurrencies.

27. *Internet and Mobile Association of India v. Reserve Bank of India,* 2020 SCC Online SC 275.

Key Arguments by Reserve Bank of India

- Cryptocurrencies were capable of being used for illegal purposes (on account of the digital anonymity that blockchain technology affords).
- Widespread use of cryptocurrencies would fundamentally undermine India's credit system and monetary stability.
- The RBI had the right to regulate banking activity (which is what the circular pertained to) as it saw fit.
- In any case, the RBI has the authority to make broad-based decisions on the economic policy of the country, and the Supreme Court has traditionally shown deference to RBI's authority.

Ruling by Supreme Court

The Supreme Court ruled that while cryptocurrencies do not constitute legal tender (either in India or in any other jurisdiction that the Supreme Court had analysed), they can function as either a medium of exchange, a unit of account, or a store of value (or some combination thereof). The RBI has the statutory authority to notify certain instruments as currencies, and (as the Supreme Court observed) it has not chosen to exercise this power with respect to cryptocurrencies. In fact, the RBI has specifically argued in the past that cryptocurrencies do not fall under the statutory definition of 'currency'. Nonetheless, the Supreme Court concluded that the manner in which cryptocurrencies are often used in India — as consideration for goods or services provided, or as a facilitator of payment between parties — constitutes an activity that falls within the RBI's regulatory purview.

Having concluded that the RBI did indeed have the power to regulate cryptocurrencies in India, the Supreme Court proceeded to evaluate the circular on its merits. While the Supreme Court rejected the argument that there had been no application of mind in the RBI's directives and that it did not find the circular to be a colourable exercise of power, the Supreme Court did ultimately conclude that the circular was a disproportionate regulatory measure.

The Supreme Court noted that the RBI is primarily responsible for the financial institutions that it is required to regulate, and that it had argued about the potential harms that cryptocurrencies could cause to those institutions. However, the RBI had failed to actually demonstrate the damage that the use of cryptocurrencies had caused to such regulated entities — given that the RBI had not identified any specific adverse impacts of cryptocurrencies on banking and financial institutions in India, and had specifically argued (both in previous regulatory guidance and during the course of arguments in the present case) that cryptocurrencies were not actually banned under Indian law.

In prohibiting regulated entities from dealing with a sector that was not subject to a statutory ban, and which had not demonstrably harmed such regulated entities, the RBI was held to have acted disproportionately, and the circular was thus set aside.

Impact of the Supreme Court Ruling

The judgement might have provided temporary relief; due to lack of regulations to regulate cryptocurrencies or virtual currencies, the financial institutions and the banking sector may not be favourably inclined towards investing in them. At this juncture, uncertainty prevails about the future of the cryptocurrency industry in India.

The wide-scale use of cryptocurrency also seems to be questionable, as the "Banning of Cryptocurrency and Regulation of Official Digital Currency Bill 2019" has been proposed with the aim to ban all private cryptocurrencies. The bill is yet to be brought to the Indian Parliament and receive approval. The bill also proposes the creation of a 'digital rupee'. We need to wait for the final bill and need to examine the implications.

The Supreme Court judgement was welcomed as it not only gave partial relief to those dealing in cryptocurrencies but also defined the RBI's powers in this context. It also urged administrators and law-makers to accept and imbibe the digital revolution and create suitable policies and a framework to encourage digital that has the impact of creating 'growth through disruption'.

Chapter 3

DIGITAL ECONOMY AND INDIAN INCOME-TAX DEVELOPMENTS

India has been responding to issues on the Digital Economy in more than one way. The Government of India amended the Income-tax Act, 1961 to bring 'Equalisation levy' and nexus theory by creating a new concept called 'Significant Economic Presence' (SEP). Further, the Central Board of Direct Taxes (CBDT) released a draft report on attribution of profits which seeks to adopt an approach completely different from the separate entity approach that is the basis of attribution of profits under Article 7(1) of Double Taxation Avoidance Agreement (DTAA).

Introduction of Equalisation levy

The Finance Act, 2016 introduced the Equalisation levy with effect from June 01, 2016, thereby introducing the concept of levy on specified e-commerce services. The scope of the levy was further widened by the Finance Act, 2020 to bring in more goods and services under its ambit.

E-commerce Committee Report[28]

The committee on taxation of e-commerce formed by the CBDT recommended introduction of the Equalisation levy for the following reasons:

- The introduction of the *'new nexus based on significant economic presence'* may not be sufficient for taxing income on the new economic nexus theory without corresponding amendments to bring such nexus under treaty laws.
- The option of bringing withholding tax on digital transactions under the Income-tax Act, 1961 will also be ineffective without corresponding changes in DTAA.

28. Available at: https://incometaxindia.gov.in/News/Report-of-Committee-on-Taxation-of-e-Commerce-Feb-2016.pdf; last accessed on July 12, 2021.

Note:

Section 90(2) of the Income-tax Act, 1961 allows the taxpayer to choose DTAA or domestic tax laws whichever is more beneficial. Hence, the committee concluded that bringing the nexus theory under the Income-tax Act 1961 or imposing withholding (WHT) on digital transactions will not be effective due to the beneficial provisions of the DTAA.

- In view of section 90(2) and India's commitment to honor its obligations under DTAA, the committee recommended a third option, which does not get covered by the DTAA, i.e., introduction of Equalisation levy under the Finance Act, 2016 and not under the Income-tax Act, 1961.
- The committee notes that this is a viable option devoid of any difficulties associated with attribution of profits.
- The committee's reasons behind the Equalisation levy are summarised in the ensuing paragraphs.[29]

In the committee's view, there is a need to consider the feasibility of adopting 'Equalisation levy' under the domestic laws of India to address the tax challenges arising from the digital economy at this stage. Adopting the levy will bring greater certainty and predictability to all the stakeholders by enabling them to take it into account the tax implications while making future business plans and deciding the pricing of products, thereby contributing to a more stable environment that would not exit in the absence of such a measure, the committee noted.

When compared with the option of including the Equalisation levy in a tax treaty, the option of incorporating it in the domestic law has significant advantages as it lends to simplicity, uniformity and consistency as well as minimises administrative and compliance costs; therefore, it is the preferred option.

- The committee recommended that the Equalisation levy should be limited to payments made for intangible services, including payments for use or right to use any intangible, digital, telecommunication or

29. Report by Committee on Taxation of E-Commerce formed by the Central Board of Direct Taxes, Department of Revenue, Ministry of Finance, Government of India, Paras 181 and 182, February, 2016 available at https://incometaxindia.gov.in/News/Report-of-Committee-on-Taxation-of-e-Commerce-Feb-2016.pdf; last accessed on July 12, 2021.

similar network; or availing any service or other benefit received from a foreign company or a person outside India, provided the services are either received, utilised, provided or performed in India, and thus have a nexus with India, irrespective of whether the payment is made by a resident or a non-resident person.

Introduction of the Equalisation levy and its subsequent expansion by the Finance Act, 2020 has created controversies on its application that are discussed below.

Is the Equalisation levy constitutionally valid?

The committee observes that[30] Equalisation levy on gross amounts of transactions or payments made for digital services is in line with the Entry 92C and 97, First List in the Seventh Schedule to the Constitution of India. The committee considers levy of service tax as a precedent to justify imposition of the Equalisation levy. Differing views exist on the constitutional validity of Equalisation levy, which are summarised below:

- Entry 92C was not notified by the Constitution, and it was omitted by the Constitution (One Hundred and First) Amendment Act, 2016. Thus, legislative sanction cannot come from Entry 92C.
- The subject matter is levy of tax on gross amount of transactions made for digital services. Entry 97 to the First List in the Seventh Schedule to the Constitution of India reads as "*Any other matter not enumerated in List II or List III including any tax not mentioned in either of those Lists*".
- Entry 97 is a residual list and the issue is whether the direct charge of taxation on digital service should come under the residual clause.
- The Supreme Court in the case of *Union of India* v. *Shri Harbhajan Singh Dhillon*[31] observed that "In the layout of such elaborate worded matters in the Lists and in the context of Article 246(1), the residuary power contained in Article 248 and Entry 97, List I must be construed

30. Report by Committee on Taxation of E-Commerce formed by the Central Board of Direct Taxes, Department of Revenue, Ministry of Finance, Government of India, Para 130, February, 2016 available at https://incometaxindia.gov.in/News/Report-of-Committee-on-Taxation-of-e-Commerce-Feb-2016.pdf; last accessed on July 12, 2021.
31. AIR 1972 SC 1061.

giving power in respect of matters not enumerated in any of the three Lists. Such a residuary power cannot, therefore, be ordinarily claimed in respect of a matter already dealt with under an Article or an entry in any one of the three lists", anything not included in List II or List III.

- In view of it, the issue is whether Central government has the power to legislate Equalisation levy on digital transaction, when the Central and State governments have legislated the GST Act, 2017 to tax digital services.
- Therefore, the constitutional validity of Equalisation levy is not free from doubt, and the committee's basis on the levy does not have legislative competence in view of dropping of Entry 92C and lack of authority under Entry 97.

Scope of the Equalisation Levy

Introduction by Finance Act, 2016

The Finance Act, 2016 introduced the Equalisation levy with effect from June 01, 2016. The scope of Equalisation, as per Finance Act, 2016, is to levy tax at 6% on consideration received or receivable by a non-resident seller from a person residing in India and carrying on business or profession, or a non-resident having a Permanent Establishment (PE) in India.

The term 'specified service' means[32] online advertisement, any provision for digital advertising space or any other facility or service for the purpose of online advertisement and includes any other service as may be notified by the Central government in this behalf.

The idea is to tax revenue generated by foreign online companies that have earned the revenue from India but do not have any business presence in the country through the Equalisation levy.

Expansion of Scope by Finance Act, 2020

The scope of the Equalisation levy was expanded through an amendment to the Finance Act, 2020. Under it, [33]2% shall be charged, as Equalisation levy, on the amount of consideration received or receivable by an ***e-commerce***

32. Section 164(h) of Chapter VIII of Finance Act, 2016.
33. Section 153(iv) of Part VI of Finance Act, 2020.

operator from an e-commerce supplier or for e-commerce services provided or facilitated to:

(i) A person resident in India.

(ii) To a non-resident in the following circumstances:

(a) Proceeds from sale of advertisement which targets customers who are residents in India or customers who access the advertisements through an internet protocol (IP) address located in India.

(b) Proceeds from sale of data collected from a person who is a resident in India or from a person who uses an IP address located in India.

(iii) To a person who buys such goods or services or both using an IP address located in India.

The term 'e-commerce operator'[34] means a *non-resident who owns, operates or manages digital or electronic facility or platform for online sale of goods or online provision of services or both.*

The term e-commerce supply or services means[35]

(i) online sale of goods owned by the e-commerce operator or

(ii) online provision of services provided by the e-commerce operator or

(iii) online sale of goods or provisions of services facilitated by the e-commerce operator or

(iv) any combination of the above.

Exceptions

The Equalisation levy of 2% is not applicable if:[36]

> The non-resident e-commerce operator, making or providing or facilitating e-commerce supply or services, has a PE in India and the supply or services are effectively connected with that PE.

34. Section 164(ca) of Chapter VIII of Finance Act, 2016 as amended by Section 153 (ii) of Finance Act, 2020.
35. Section 164(cb) of Chapter VIII of Finance Act, 2016 as amended by Section 153 (ii) of Finance Act, 2020.
36. Section 165A(2) of Finance Act, 2016 as amended by Section 153 (ii) of Finance Act, 2020.

If levied under Section 165, i.e., EL under the Equalisation Levy Rules, 2016.

Sales or turnover or gross receipts from the e-commerce supply or services made or provided are less than ₹ 2 crore during the financial year.

Practical Issues: Scope of e-commerce supply or services

The scope of e-commerce supply or services has widened significantly. The earlier levy, i.e., levy by Finance Act, 2016 was predominantly meant for B2B (Business to Business) transactions. Under the expanded scope on Equalisation levy by Finance Act, 2020, B2C (Business to Consumer) transactions also fall within the levy's purview. These include not only e-commerce companies and/or e-commerce operators but also manufacturing and retail companies as well as hospitality and tourism firms that make sales or provide services using e-commerce.

For example:

A brick-and-mortar-company engaged in manufacturing of goods outside India by a foreign company or a non-resident, who sells goods in India through their website is subject to Equalisation levy.

If a book publisher sells books through their website to a customer in India, they are subject to Equalisation levy.

If a person in India makes a hotel booking outside India through the hotel's website, then the hotel pays the Equalisation levy in India.

Earlier, the above companies were not subject to tax in India even if they did not have a PE in India. The expanded scope of the Equalisation levy, by Finance Act, 2020, subjects these companies to pay the Equalisation levy, even though they are not subject to tax in India under the normal provisions of the Income-tax Act. However, by virtue of section 165A(2), the above companies will not be subject to the levy if:

If they have a PE in India, and the sale of goods or provision of services is effectively connected with that PE.

The sales or turnover or gross receipts from the e-commerce supply or services rendered in India do not exceed ₹ 2 crore in a year.

Withholding of Tax and Equalisation Levy

Extending the scope of Equalisation levy, by the Finance Act, 2020, has brought to the fore the issue of which tax, Withholding Tax (WHT) or Equalisation levy will be applicable while carrying out certain e-commerce transactions. In this section, we will examine some of those issues.

WHT and Equalisation Levy on Provision of Services

E-commerce services like online purchase of software may not be subject to WHT but may incur Equalisation levy if they are facilitated by an e-commerce operator.

WHT and Equalisation Levy on Purchase of Software

Whether downloading of software is subject to WHT or not is a debatable issue. Lack of clarity persists on the applicability of WHT on software until the Supreme Court delivers its verdict on the matter. Regardless of it, if an Indian resident purchases software online from a foreign company, will the latter have to pay Equalisation levy in India, subject to the exceptions in section 165A(2)?

Section 10(50) of the Income-tax Act, 1961 provides that any income from any specified services provided, after the notification of Finance Act, 2016, or arising from any e-commerce supply of goods or services made or provided or facilitated on or after April 01, 2016 are chargeable to Equalisation levy.

Section 10(50) clearly specifies that the amount on sale of goods or services, subject to Equalisation levy under Finance Act, 2016, is exempted from income under the provisions of this section. Hence, it may be possible to take a position that a transaction subject to Equalisation levy is not chargeable to WHT.

Services between non-residents[37]

A non-resident e-commerce operator rendering services to another non-resident would fall within the charge of Equalisation levy, under the following two 'specified circumstances':

37. Courtesy Rashmi Maskara and Yatik Kothari.

I. Sale of advertisement

II. Sale of data

Thus, any other type of e-commerce supply or service to another non-resident should be outside the scope of Equalisation levy, but this is not so. Services provided by one non-resident to another non-resident even though not falling within specified circumstances and therefore outside the scope of Equalisation levy, would fall within the ambit of such levy, if they qualify as facilitation in the online supply of goods or services[38].

In this regard, let us consider a scenario where:

- An e-commerce operator, 'A', is engaged in online sale of goods or services to Indian customers; and
- 'A' is availing the services of another e-commerce operator, 'B', for this purpose.

In such a case, the consideration received by 'B' would also be subject to Equalisation levy if their services to 'A' qualify as facilitation. Accordingly, it becomes important to understand the meaning and scope of the term 'facilitate'.

The term 'facilitate' has not been defined under the Finance Act, 2016. Reference is made to Integrated Goods and Service Tax Act, 2017, wherein the phrase 'facilitate' is used in relation to an intermediary service[39]. 'Facilitate' is a very wide term as every commerce and trade is engaged either in supply of goods/services or in services that facilitate supply of goods/services. Accepting this, in 2019, the Maharashtra Appellate Authority for Advance Ruling for Goods and Services Tax held that back-office support services would qualify as intermediary services[40]. It was concluded that such services were in the nature of facilitation for the supply of goods. The ruling caused uproar in the ITeS sector; currently, however, there is no clarity on this subject.

---

38. Section 164(cb)(ii) read with section 165A(i)/(iii) of the Finance Act.
39. Intermediary is defined to mean a broker, an agent or any other person, by whatever name called, who arranges or facilitates the supply of goods or services or both, or securities, between two or more persons, but does not include a person who supplies such goods or services or both or securities on his own account.
40. *Re*: *Vservglobal Private Limited,* Order No. MAH/AAAR/SS-RJ/22/2018-19 dated 26 February 26, 2019.

This approach towards interpreting the term 'facilitate' under Equalisation levy would have far-reaching implications. It leads to the obvious question as to what qualifies as 'facilitation' of online sale of goods and services to invoke Equalisation levy. Alternatively, whether they can be 'services' not falling under 'specified circumstances', hence not chargeable to Equalisation levy.

To arrive at a conclusion, various factors need to be considered such as agreement between the non-resident e-commerce operator and the non-resident service provider; consideration agreed between the parties; flow of consideration from India; accounting entries, whether any user-interface is present between 'B' and the Indian customers among others.

If the services of 'B' qualify as facilitation, then it may lead to taxation in the hands of multiple e-commerce operators despite the fact that the entire transaction value is already subject to Equalisation levy on online sale of goods/services in the hands of 'A'. The issue broadly arises because the law does not provide for any sort of exemption from levy of Equalisation levy.

Equalisation Levy and Significant Economic Presence

The Finance Act, 2018 introduced the concept of 'Significant Economic Presence' (SEP) in the Income-tax Act, 1961 for taxation of non-residents in India by expanding the scope definition of "business connection". Explanation 2A to section 9 of Income Tax Act, 1961, inserted with effect from April 01, 2020, expands the scope of business connection to include SEP. Section 9(1)(i) defines SEP as:

(a) transaction in respect of any goods, services or property carried out by a non-resident in India, including the provision of download of data or software in India, if the aggregate of payments arising from such transaction or transactions during the previous year exceeds such amount as may be prescribed; or

(b) systematic and continuous soliciting of business activities or engaging in interaction with such number of users as may be prescribed, in India through digital means.

Provided that the transactions or activities shall constitute significant economic presence in India, whether or not-

(i) the agreement for such transactions or activities is entered into in India or

(ii) the non-resident has a residence or place of business in India or

(iii) the non-resident renders services in India.

Provided further that only so much of income as is attributable to the transactions or activities referred to in clause (a) or clause (b) shall be deemed to accrue or arise in India.[41]

Is there any overlap between SEP and Equalisation levy?

Section 10(50) of the Income-tax Act, 1961 provides that any income from any specified services provided after the notification of Finance Act, 2016, or arising from any e-commerce supply of goods or services made or provided or facilitated on or after April 01, 2016 are chargeable to Equalisation levy.

The wordings of section 10(50) make it clear that the amount on sale of goods or services which are subject to Equalisation levy under the Finance Act, 2016 is exempted from income under the provisions of section 10(50). Therefore, one can conclude that there is no overlap. Further, section 165A(2) provides exception that the non-resident is not subject to Equalisation levy if the non-resident has a PE in India. Hence if the non-resident has a PE in India due to SEP, then a position can be taken that transaction is not subject to Equalisation levy under section 165A of Finance Act, 2016.

Significant Economic Presence (SEP)

Explanation 2A to section 9(1)(i) of the Income-tax Act, 1961 defines SEP[42]. In view of this definition, activities of e-commerce companies can be brought under the purview of SEP. Since the definition of PE under the DTAA has not been modified yet, the expanded scope may not have the desired impact as the provisions of DTAA or domestic tax law, whichever is more beneficial, shall be applicable.

Imposition of domestic withholding tax

Section 194-O, introduced by Finance Act, 2020 with effect from October 01, 2020, imposes WHT on domestic transactions between e-commerce participants and e-commerce operator on sale of goods or provision of services.

---

41. Explanation 2A to Section 9(1)(i) of Income-tax Act, 1961.
42. Refer to 'Equalisation Levy and Significant Economic Presence' above.

Under the provisions of this section, where sale of goods or provision of services of an e-commerce participant is facilitated by an e-commerce operator, through its digital or electronic facility or platform, the e-commerce operator is required to withhold tax at 1% on payments made to the e-commerce participant. The obligation to deduct tax at source by e-commerce operator arises either at the time of creation of liability or at the time of payment whichever is earlier.

The obligation to deduct tax at source by e-commerce operator is not required if the gross amount of sale of goods or services or both does not exceed ₹5 lakh per annum, and the e-commerce operator furnishes his PAN or Aadhaar number to the e-commerce operator.

The obligation to deduct tax at source arises on the e-commerce operator only in respect of sale of goods or provision of services by the e-commerce participant, but it is not applicable for hosting of advertisement or services, which are not in connection with sale of goods or provision of services by the e-commerce participant.

For the purpose of application of section 194-O, let us look at the definitions:

> Electronic commerce means the supply of goods or services or both including digital products, over digital or electronic network.
>
> E-commerce operator means a person who owns, operates or manages digital or electronic facility or platform for electronic commerce.
>
> E-commerce participant means a person resident in India selling goods or providing services or both, including digital products, through digital or electronic facility or platform for electronic commerce.
>
> Services includes 'fees for technical services' and 'fees for professional services' as defined in the Explanation to Section 194J.

Understanding of Section 194-O

1. ***Currently, in an e-commerce transaction, what is the withholding tax applicable? How is it discharged?***

   Currently, the e-commerce operator earns a commission for sale of products on his platform. This commission earned by the e-commerce operator is subject to a withholding tax under section 194H. However, in a typical e-commerce transaction, the e-commerce operator collects the money for facilitation of goods and services on the platform (via nodal account) and then deposits it to the e-commerce participant. It is the liability of the e-commerce participant to discharge the withholding tax under section 194H. In a practical scenario, the seller deposits TDS (tax deduction at source) under section 194H as commission and then on production of proof of deposit, the e-commerce operator will reimburse the value. There is a reference to this type of arrangement in the 1991 circular issued when the section was introduced.

2. What does the new provision entail?

Under the new provisions, the e-commerce operator is required to withhold tax on the consideration received for sale of goods from the customers at the time when such consideration is in turn passed on to the e-commerce participant. The rate of withholding tax is 1% (reduced to 0.75% as a part of pandemic measures). Given the withholding on commission and the e-commerce facilitation itself are on two different legs of the transactions, both there will be 2 levies.

3. Under the new provisions, if the e-commerce operator fails to withhold tax under section 194-O, will there be disallowance under the law?

In the case of non-deduction of tax under section 194-O, there should not be any disallowance for the e-commerce operation, given that the payment made by the e-commerce operator to the e-commerce participant is not an expenditure for the e-commerce operator. Section 40A applies to cases where the person liable to deduct tax claims an expenditure.

4. What are the e-commerce sales scenarios on which withholding tax is expected?

The provisions of section 194-O applies to a transaction for facilitation of e-commerce goods or services. There can be 2 scenarios:

(iii) The facilitation happens on the e-commerce portal — the provisions of section 194-O is triggered

(iv) The e-commerce operator merely advertises other brands/ portals and the transaction is concluded on the portal of the other player - Then the provisions of 194-O should not be attracted as the second player will only be advertising and withholding the tax. If the second e-commerce player is a seller himself, section 194-O will not be attracted. However, where the second e-commerce player itself is an e-commerce operator, then he will have to undertake section 194-O compliance for transactions on his portal.

Let us try to understand the provisions of this section through an example

K.Cart.com is an e-commerce operator, selling goods to customers through its website or portal. K.Cart.com purchases these goods from somebody and then sells them to customers. In addition, K.Cart.com allows other sellers to use its portal for selling goods. For example, A Pvt. Ltd sells watches/books through K.Cart.com.

Customer 'X' visits K.Cart.com, places an order to buy goods of A Pvt. Ltd and 'X' uses his/her credit card to make payment. In the next step to this transaction, the merchant bank of 'X' customer pays the amount to K.Cart.com who, in turn, will deduct commission for providing the online platform to A Pvt. Ltd before making the payment.

Let us apply Section 194-O, which imposes withholding tax, to the above example

K.Cart.com – is an e-commerce operator

A Pvt. Ltd – is an e-commerce participant

K.Cart.com being an e-commerce operator will have to deduct tax at source at applicable rates on the gross amount payable to A Pvt. Ltd. The obligation to deduct tax at source on K.Cart.com arises either at the time of payment or creation of liability whichever is earlier.

However, K.Cart.com is under no obligation to deduct tax at source:

- If the gross value of consideration payable by K.Cart.com to A Pvt. Ltd does not exceed ₹ 5 lakh in a year for sale of goods or services or both.

- If the value of consideration is less than ₹ 5 lakh a Pvt. Ltd is required to furnish PAN (permanent account number) or Aadhar Card number to K.Cart.com, failing which K.Cart.com is under obligation to deduct WHT on payments to A Pvt. Ltd even if the consideration is less than ₹ 5 lakh.

The same provisions will be applicable if A Pvt. Ltd offers its services. For this purpose, services mean fee for technical services or fee for professional services as defined under section 194J.

Professional services mean services rendered by a person in the course of providing legal, medical, engineering, architectural, accountancy, technical consultancy, interior design or advertising services as notified.

Fee for technical services[43] means any consideration (including any lump sum consideration) for the rendering of any managerial, technical or consultancy services (including the services of provision of technical personnel) but does not include consideration for any construction, assembly, mining or like project undertaken by the recipient or consideration which would be income of the recipient chargeable under the head 'salaries'.

Failure to charge withholding tax by K.Cart.com to A Pvt. Ltd will attract consequences under provision of section 40(a)(ia), whereby 30 percent of the amount payable to A Pvt. Ltd will not be eligible for deduction by the e-commerce operator.

Amendments by Finance Act, 2021

(a) Section 163(3) of Finance Act, 2016 amended to eliminate ambiguity on dual implications of Royalty/FTS and Equalisation levy along with consequential amendment to section 10(50) of the Income-tax Act, 1961 ;

(b) Section 164(cb) of Finance Act, 2016 amended to provide that any 'online element' of a transaction may trigger Equalisation levy;

(c) Section 165A(3) of Finance Act, 2016 amended to define term 'consideration' for sale of goods/provision of services;

43. Explanation 2 to Section 9(1)(vii) of Income-tax Act, 1961.

Executive Summary:

Sl. No.	Amendment	Implications	Remarks
1	*Amendment to section 163(3) of Finance Act, 2016 read with amendment to section 10(50) of Income-tax Act, 1961*	*Payment taxable as royalty/fees for technical service would now <u>not attract Equalisation levy</u>* *Income-tax Act, 1961 will now override Equalisation levy*	*Characterisation of payment as royalty/Fees for Technical Services (FTS) becomes critical.* *If payment towards royalty/ fees for technical service is exempted under a tax treaty, Equalisation levy could still apply* *Since the amendment is retrospective, any potential refund could be explored*
2	*Amendment to section 164(cb) of Finance Act, 2016*	*Acceptance of offer for sale/placing of Purchase Order (PO)/ acceptance of the PO/ payment of consideration/supply of goods/ services – any one of these activities performed online could attract Equalisation levy*	*Disintegrating sales lifecycle and identifying if any of the activity was performed online is a key action item in evaluating impact of Equalisation levy.* *Differences in interpretation of whether a particular activity triggered Equalisation levy could lead to litigations*
3	*Amendment to section 165A(3) of Finance Act, 2016*	*Equalisation levy ought to be levied on gross consideration in the hands of facilitating entities as well, who*	*This amendment is retrospective in nature. Hence, businesses ought to revisit their exposure to the levy so as to*

Sl. No.	Amendment	Implications	Remarks
		will receive the consideration for goods/ services, even if not owned by them	*enable them to obtain PAN to pay the levy or in cases where the levy has been deposited for earlier quarters, to true up the levy in the last quarter payment*

Detailed analysis of Finance Act, 2021

A. *Amendment to section 163(3) of Finance Act, 2016 and section 10(50) of the Income-tax Act, 1961 to eliminate ambiguity on dual implications of Royalty/FTS and Equalisation levy*

A proviso is inserted to section 163(3) of Finance Act, 2016 to state that the consideration liable for Equalisation levy shall not include consideration, which is taxable as royalty or FTS in India as per Income Tax Act, 1961, read with tax treaties.

This amendment is effective retrospectively from April 01, 2020.

Earlier, no exemption from income tax was provided on payment of Equalisation levy for those taxpayers making payments in the nature of royalties/FTS. This resulted in payment of taxes under both Income-tax Act, 1961 (in form of WHT) as well as Finance Act, 2016 (in form of Equalisation levy).

The amendment has now settled this anomaly by carving out payments in the nature of royalties/FTS from the ambit of Equalisation levy. As a result, taxpayers would now need to seek refund of amounts already paid during the period this anomaly existed (i.e., in FY 2020-21).

Also, hereinafter, characterisation of a payment as royalties/FTS becomes even more significant. If the payment is taxable as royalties/ FTS, it is liable to income-tax and the taxpayer may claim foreign tax credit in their home jurisdiction. If the payment is not in the nature of royalties/FTS, Equalisation levy would have to be paid on the same.

It is also interesting to note that the exemption from Equalisation levy is available if a service is taxable as royalty/FTS under the Income Tax Act, 1961, read with the relevant tax treaty. Therefore, if a payment is taxable as royalty/FTS under the Act, but treaty benefit is available, the taxpayer will may still need to pay Equalisation levy.

Consequential amendments are also made to section 10(50) of Income-tax Act, 1961 to modify exemption provided to income which suffers Equalisation levy, to exclude income chargeable to tax as royalty/FTS under Income-tax Act, 1961/tax treaties.

B. Amendment to section 164(cb) of Finance Act, 2016 to provide that any 'online element' of a transaction may trigger Equalisation levy

An explanation is inserted to section 164(cb) of Finance Act, 2016 to provide that for the purposes of section 164(cb), 'online sale of goods'/ provision of services' shall include <u>one or more</u> of the following online activities namely:—

- acceptance of offer for sale; or
- placing of purchase order; or
- acceptance of the purchase order; or
- payment of consideration; or
- supply of goods or provision of services, partly or wholly.

This amendment is effective retrospectively from April 01, 2020.

Earlier, in absence of a precise definition of online sale of goods/ provision of services, varied interpretations were possible on whether 'sale/providing service' would only include cases where the sale was concluded online i.e., including the delivery leg, or either conclusion of the sales contract or delivery or both or even stages precedent to contract conclusion. This ambiguity is settled by the above amendment which clearly provides that conducting <u>any one or more</u> of the above activities would result in sale/service being considered as provided online, thereby triggering Equalisation levy provisions.

In light of the above amendment, fragmenting the entire sales lifecycle and testing the provisions of Equalisation levy is key action for several industries. It is quite likely that taxpayers may face challenges in complying with the wide ambit of Equalisation levy, leading to possible litigations.

C. *Amendment to section 165A(3) of Finance Act, 2016 to define term 'consideration' for sale of goods/provision of services*

The amendment has sought to provide an inclusive definition of the term 'consideration' received or receivable from e-commerce supply or services. It shall now include—

- Consideration for sale of goods irrespective of whether the e-commerce operator owns the goods; or
- Consideration for provisions of services irrespective of whether the service is provided or facilitated by the e-commerce operator

However, the consideration <u>shall not include</u> consideration for sale of goods/provision of services:

- by a person resident in India;
- by a PE of a non-resident in India if such sale is effectively connected with such PE.

This amendment is effective retrospectively from April 01, 2020.

Earlier, there were divergent views on the base amount on which Equalisation levy should apply in cases where the consideration was received by payment collection agents or marketplaces and not the NR himself. The issue was whether the consideration for sale of goods/ services received by the collection agents or marketplaces ought to be liable to Equalisation levy in their hands or not; whether Equalisation levy should apply on the gross consideration or only on the fee charged by such marketplace/agent for their service.

The above amendment has settled such ambiguity to state that consideration for sale of goods/services is taxable even if the e-commerce operator is not the owner of goods/services. Therefore, if payment gateways/marketplaces were up until now offering only the net consideration to Equalisation levy, they will henceforth need to compute Equalisation levy on gross consideration.

Since this amendment is retrospective in nature, it is imperative for businesses to revisit their exposure to the levy so as to enable them to obtain Indian tax registration to pay the levy or in cases where the levy has been deposited for earlier quarters, to true up the levy in the last quarter payment due on March 31. The practical challenges around this amendment would nevertheless require detailed discussion.

Impact of US Trade and Commerce Report on Equalisation Levy

On June 02, 2020, the United States Trade Representative [USTR] initiated an investigation on India's Equalisation levy under section 301 of the US Trade Act, 1974. Other countries under investigation include Italy, Turkey and the United Kingdom. The USTR carried out its investigation of India's EL over the course of several months and issued a report dated January 06, 2021, pursuant to the investigation [the Report[44]].

Event leading to investigation by the USTR

While the global consensus is yet to be reached, India has introduced Equalisation levy, at two points in time as of today, among other unilateral measures. In 2016, India adopted a 6% Equalisation levy, applicable on gross revenue received by non-residents for online advertisements and related services provided to Indian residents. The Indian party availing such services are required to withhold and remit the levy to the Indian government.

However, the 2016 Equalisation levy is not the focus of the US investigation. Rather, it is the new Equalisation levy introduced by India in 2020 that is the focus of this investigation. The new levy came into effect at a very short notice and the fundamental aspects of this levy, such as the scope of services covered, companies impacted, etc. are yet to be clarified while the mechanics of how to pay the levy was rolled out in October 2020.

India's Equalisation levy or Digital Services Tax [DST]

The newly introduced Equalisation levy applies at 2% on consideration received by foreign e-commerce operators from e-commerce supply/service made or provided or facilitated by it:

---

44. Available at: https://ustr.gov/sites/default/files/files/reports/2021/2021%20Special%20301%20Report%20(final).pdf; last accessed on July 12, 2021.

- To a person resident in India; or
- To a non-resident in 'specified circumstances'; or
- To a person who buys such goods or services or both using internet protocol ["IP"] address located in India.

"Specified circumstances" means:

- Sale of advertisement, which targets a customer, who is resident in India or a customer who accesses the advertisement though IP address located in India; and
- Sale of data, collected from a person who is resident in India or from a person who uses IP address located in India.

However, Equalisation levy is not applicable in following cases:

- ➢ where the e-commerce operator has a PE in India and such e-commerce supply or services is effectively connected with such PE; or
- ➢ where Equalisation levy is leviable on online advertisement and related activities in terms of the 2016 Equalisation levy provision; or
- ➢ sales, turnover or gross receipts, of the e-commerce operator from the e-commerce supply or services made or provided or facilitated is less than INR 20 million (USD 267,000 approx.) during the financial year.

The Equalisation levy provision defines "e-commerce supply or services" as:

(i) online sale of goods owned by the e-commerce operator; or

(ii) online provision of services provided by the e-commerce operator; or

(iii) online sale of goods or provision of services or both, facilitated by the e- commerce operator; or

(iv) any combination of activities listed in clause (i), (ii) or clause (iii).

This definition is extremely broad. Thus, subject to above exceptions, Equalisation levy applies to revenues received by a wide range of non-Indian digital service providers for a broad array of digital services.

Legal basis for USTR's Investigation

The investigation was initiated under section 301 of the US Trade Act, 1974.

Section 301 sets out legal basis for three types of acts, policies, or practices of a foreign country that are actionable: (i) trade agreement violations; (ii) acts, policies or practices that are unjustifiable (defined as those that are inconsistent with U.S. international legal rights) and burden or restrict U.S. Commerce; and (iii) acts, policies or practices that are unreasonable or discriminatory and burden or restrict U.S. Commerce.

If the USTR determines that the act, policy, or practice falls within any of the three categories of actionable conduct under section 301, they must also determine what action needs to be taken.

[45]Actions authorized under section 301 include:

(i) suspending, withdrawing, or preventing the application of benefits of trade agreement concessions;

(ii) imposing duties, fees, or other import restrictions on the goods or services of the foreign country;

(iii) entering into binding agreements that commit the foreign country to eliminate or phase out the offending conduct or to provide compensatory trade benefits; or

(iv) restricting or denying the issuance of service sector authorizations, which are federal permits or other authorizations needed to supply services in some sectors in the United States.

USTR's investigation of India's EL

The investigation involves determinations of whether India's Equalisation levy is actionable under section 301 of the US Trade Act, 1974, and if so, what action needs to be taken. With respect to actionability, the investigation focused on discrimination against U.S. companies, and divergence from reasonable tax policy i.e., principles reflected in the U.S. tax system and the international tax system, such as extraterritorial reach and taxing revenue rather than income.

---

45. Available at: https://ustr.gov/sites/default/files/enforcement/301Investigations/Report%20on%20India%E2%80%99s%20Digital%20Services%20Tax.pdf; last accessed on July 12, 2021, pp 8.

The USTR conducted consultations on November 05, 2020, with the Indian government. It also provided the public and other interested persons an opportunity to present their views and perspectives on the India's Equalisation levy. The USTR received comments majorly towards India's Equalisation levy and the Report[46] of the USTR submits that a substantial majority supported a positive finding on actionability of India's EL. The report further mentions that commenters provided evidence and argumentation supporting actionability that, *inter alia*, India's Equalisation levy discriminates against U.S. companies that it is unreasonable and that it burdens or restricts U.S. commerce.

The statute defines an "unreasonable" measure as one that "while not necessarily in violation of, or inconsistent with, the international legal rights of the United States is otherwise unfair and inequitable." As per USTR, tax measures that fail to comport with established principles of international taxation may be considered "unfair and inequitable," and thus, unreasonable under section 301.

Reasons for considering India's EL actionable

- Equalisation levy applies to only "non-resident" operators (including U.S. companies) and not to Indian entities.
- Only digital services are targeted, and not the same or similar services provided non-digitally, thus the India's Equalisation levy disproportionately impacts U.S. firms, which are market leaders in the digital services sector. The U.S. position—as expressed in international fora—is that any changes to the international tax system should apply across business models and not attempt to 'ring-fence' the digital economy.
- The report mentions that Indian Government acknowledged that's its EL included a low threshold. Further, India's Equalisation levy does not contain a global revenue threshold.
- Although the Equalisation levy potentially applies to all non-Indian digital services companies, in practice, the majority of companies subject to the tax will be U.S. firms. USTR's analysis identified 119 companies likely subject to the India's Equalisation levy, of which 86

46. *Ibid.*

(72%) are U.S. companies, whereas the next most common nationalities are China and the United Kingdom with seven companies each, France with six companies, and Japan with five. No Indian companies appear on this list due to their explicit exemption from the Equalisation levy.

- India's Equalisation levy applies to revenue derived from nearly any type of digital activity that generates revenue subject to exceptions. As per USTR, this includes categories of digital services that are not taxable under most other countries' digital services taxes, such as streaming video services, digital sale of a company's own goods, cloud services, and the provision of software-as-a-service.
- The hurried process produced a law that stakeholders have found to be unclear and underdeveloped. These ambiguities contravene the core international taxation principle of tax "certainty".
- Stakeholders have identified a number of ambiguities regarding the scope of services subject to the levy; the universe of companies liable; the applicability of the levy to intragroup transactions and re-seller/distributor arrangements; the proper method of calculating a company's tax base; the applicability of the levy to the sale of advertisements between non- residents; the applicability of the levy to the sale of data between non-residents; and when tax liability begins to accrue under the levy. The Indian government have been approached for clarification, but no clarification has been released yet.
- Its targets revenues unconnected to a physical presence in India that contravenes prevailing international tax principles. Rather than limiting India's Equalisation levy applicability to companies with PE in India, this levy applies only to companies without PE in India. This, as per USTR, is not consistent with international tax principles.
- Equalisation levy's application to revenue rather than income is inconsistent with prevailing principles of international taxation, which recognize income, not gross revenue as an appropriate basis for taxation.
- USTR's analysis indicates that U.S. companies, in the aggregate, may face tax payments in excess of US $ 30 million per year under this

levy. This issue is particularly salient given that many digital companies, including many U.S. companies expected to be subject to Equalisation levy —are low- or zero-margin businesses.

➢ USTR's analysis also indicates that there would be substantial administrative burdens in terms of compliance costs and re-engineering the internal systems.

➢ U.S. companies that pay the Equalisation levy in India will still be subject to U.S. corporate income tax, creating two layers of taxation. Avoiding double taxation of this sort is the focus of prominent model tax treaties as well as the U.S.-India Tax Treaty. Furthermore, in some circumstances, companies subject to the Equalisation levy could face <u>triple taxation</u>. Example provided in the report is extracted below:

> "a French digital advertising company that directs advertising to Indian users. That company may be liable to pay the French digital services tax, the Indian DST, and French income tax on the revenue from that single advertising placement. Although the United States has no digital services tax, U.S. companies could nonetheless face triple taxation risk if they own subsidiaries in countries with national digital services taxes. The public comments USTR received highlighted the potential for triple taxation pursuant to the DST.[47]"

Conclusion pursuant to investigation

Based on the above, the investigation supports a finding that: India's Equalisation levy discriminates against U.S. companies; it is inconsistent with international tax principles and therefore unreasonable; and it burdens or restricts U.S. commerce on following basis:

- **Discrimination:** The Report states that discrimination takes two main forms: (1) explicitly targeting non-domestic firms, while exempting Indian companies; and (2) taxing digital services, but not taxing the same or similar services provided non-digitally. Both practices are discriminatory, and both have outsized impact on U.S. digital services firms.

---

47. Report on India's Digital Services Tax, January 6, 2021 pp 27, available at: *https://ustr.gov/sites/default/files/enforcement/301Investigations/Report%20on%20India%E2%80%99s%20Digital%20Services%20Tax.pdf* ; last accessed on July 12, 2021.

- **Unreasonable:** The Report states that three aspects of India's Equalisation levy are inconsistent with international tax principles, and thus, unreasonable under section 301: the Equalisation levy's failure to provide tax certainty to stakeholders; extraterritorial application; and application to revenue rather than income.
- **Burdensome or Restrictive:** The report states that Equalisation levy burdens U.S. commerce by, *inter alia*: obligating U.S. companies to pay tens of millions of dollars in new taxes; taxing an unusually broad group of digital services; forcing U.S. companies to undertake costly compliance measures; and subjecting U.S. companies to double taxation[48].

India's comments to the USTR in the investigation

- India stated that Equalisation levy is not discriminatory; but on the contrary seeks to ensure a level-playing field with respect to e-commerce activities undertaken by entities resident in India, and those that are not resident in India, or do not have a PE in India. It was also clarified that the Equalisation levy was applied only prospectively, and has no extra-territorial application, since it is based on sales occurring in the territory of India through digital means.
- India based e-commerce operators are already subject to taxes in India for revenue generated from Indian market. However, in the absence of the Equalisation levy, non-resident e-commerce operators (not having any PE in India but significant economic presence) are not required to pay taxes in respect of the consideration received in the e-commerce supply or services made in the Indian market.
- The threshold for this levy is ₹ 2 crores, which is very moderate and applies equally to all e-commerce operators across the globe having business in India. The levy does not discriminate against any U.S. companies, as it applies equally to all non-resident e-commerce operators, irrespective of their country of residence.

---

48. Report on India's Digital Services Tax, January 6, 2021 available at: *https://ustr.gov/sites/default/files/enforcement/301Investigations/Report%20on%20India%E2%80%99s%20Digital%20Services%20Tax.pdf*; last accessed on July 12, 2021.

- Equalisation levy was one of the methods suggested by 2015 OECD/G20 Report on Action 1 of BEPS[49] Project which was aimed at tackling the taxation challenges arising out of digitization of the economy. The purpose of the Equalization levy is to ensure fair competition, reasonableness and exercise the ability of governments to tax businesses that have a close nexus with the Indian market through their digital operations.

Though India has given a strong defence for the introduction of Equalisation levy, yet as explained in the earlier paragraphs the Introduction of Equalisation levy by Indian government certainly is not free from debate on the Constitutional Validity and also violation of International Principles[50].

Conclusion

As digital becomes the norm in the 'new normal' world, the expansion of digital economy and the consequent enlargement of the scope of the Indian income tax to impose Equalisation levy and domestic withholding tax has challenges both at the implementation and administration levels. We hope the issues arising on the application of these provisions are addressed by the CBDT for a smooth, fair, and impartial implementation of the taxes.

49. Available at: https://www.oecd.org/tax/beps/beps-actions/action1/; last accessed on July 12, 2021.

50. India's response to Section 301 Report of U.S. on Equalisation Levy available at https://pib.gov.in/Pressreleaseshare.aspx?PRID=1686865; last accessed on July 12, 2021.

Chapter 4

INTERNATIONAL DEVELOPMENTS ON TAXATION OF DIGITAL ECONOMY AND INDIA'S PERSPECTIVE

This chapter analyses the impact of OECD (Organisation for Economic Co-operation and Development)/G20 BEPS[51] project in offering solutions to governments of different countries to bridge the gaps in existing international tax rules by adopting results from the BEPS (Base Erosion and Profit Shifting) project into bilateral tax treaties globally, so as to check the opportunity for tax avoidance by multinational corporations. It also reviews India's perspective on BEPS, especially with regard to taxation of digital economy.

Multilateral Treaty Agreements

Multilateral treaty agreements are an outcome of the BEPS project undertaken by the OECD and G20 countries. The Multilateral Convention[52], an outcome of the project, aims to implement measures to prevent BEPS (i.e., tax planning strategies that exploit gaps and mismatches in tax rules to artificially shift profits to low or no-tax locations where there is little or no economic activity, resulting in little or no tax being paid) by offering solutions for governments to bridge the gaps in existing international tax rules. India is one of the members of the BEPS project that has identified 15 Actions to address BEPS in a comprehensive manner.[53]

Globally there are more than 3000 bilateral treaties, and the Multilateral Treaty Agreements provide a mechanism for each country to adopt the changes arising out of the BEPS project without renegotiating or amending bilateral treaties — which could be time consuming and have its own set of

51. Available at:https://www.oecd.org/tax/beps/flyer-inclusive-framework-on-beps.pdf; last accessed on July 11, 2021.
52. Available at: https://www.oecd.org/tax/treaties/multilateral-convention-to-implement-tax-treaty-related-measures-to-prevent-beps.htm; last accessed on July 11,2021.
53. Ministry of Finance, 'Ratification by India of the Multilateral Convention to Implement Tax Treaty Related Measures to Prevent Base Erosion and Profit Shifting' *Press Information Bureau – Government of India*, June 12, 2019.

negotiation challenges — with each of the treaty partner countries. The Multilateral Treaty came into force on July 01, 2018, following the deposit of ratification instrument by a fifth jurisdiction (viz. Slovenia) with the OECD Secretariat.

Structure of Multilateral Agreements

The structure of the Multilateral Agreements (MLA), consisting of 39 Articles, is explained briefly below[54]:

- Articles 1 and 2 define the scope of Multilateral Instrument (MLI) and the interpretation of terms used therein
- Articles 3–17 deal with BEPS tax treaty measures
- Articles 18–26 cover provisions related to mandatory binding arbitration
- Articles 27–39 contain procedural provisions such as provisions relevant to adoption and implementation of the MLI including ratification, entry into force and entry into effect dates, withdrawal, and so forth
- Each party to the MLI must notify tax treaties to which the MLI provisions would apply. The MLI provisions would apply to a tax treaty only if both parties notify it as Covered Tax Agreement (CTA)
- For a specific bilateral tax treaty, MLI would take effect after both parties to a CTA have deposited their ratification instruments with the OECD Secretariat.
- MLI would modify application of all CTAs at least to the extent of implementation of following minimum standards, viz.:
    - Counter treaty abuse (through Article 6 — purpose of CTA, and Article 7 — prevention of treaty abuse)
    - Improve dispute resolution (through Article 16 — mutual agreement procedure)
- Flexibility to implement BEPS tax treaty measures in various ways: The choice to apply optional and alternative provisions

54. Multilateral Instrument (MLI), "Ratification Impact on Indian tax treaties", published by Deloitte in August 2019, available at https://www2.deloitte.com/content/dam/Deloitte/in/Documents/tax/in-tax-multilateral-instrument-ratification-noexp.pdf; last accessed on July 11,2021.

- Reservations to opt out of provisions or parts of provisions that are not minimum standards (either for all CTAs, or select CTAs)

Multilateral Agreements – Impact on India

India's provisional list of CTA covers its treaties with 93 countries, which represent virtually all of its comprehensive tax treaties. Since the Multilateral Convention does not apply to Limited treaties dealing with shipping, air transport or social security, such treaties are not covered in India's list.

Many of India's important treaty partners have signed the Multilateral Convention. These include the United Kingdom, Canada, Australia, Belgium, Finland, France, Germany, Cyprus, Singapore, the Netherlands, Luxembourg, Japan, South Africa, and Ireland.

Key countries that have so far not signed the Multilateral Convention include the United States, Brazil, Malaysia, Thailand and several countries of the Middle East including Saudi Arabia, United Arab Emirates, Oman and Qatar. The Convention itself continues to remain open for signatures and more countries are expected to sign it in the coming months.

Most of India's important treaty partners have also provisionally notified their treaties with India as CTA. These include Cyprus, Singapore, the Netherlands, Australia, Luxembourg, the United Kingdom, Sweden, Canada, France, Ireland and Japan. Thus, subject to the notifications, reservations and options discussed below, the provisions of India's treaties with these countries will stand modified by the Multilateral Convention.

Important countries like Germany and Mauritius are yet to notify DTAA (Double Taxation Avoidance Agreement) with India as a part of Covered Tax Agreement. *Unless Germany and Mauritius notify their DTAA treaties with India as part of CTA, the MLA will not affect India's existing treaties with Germany and Mauritius.*

Multilateral Treaty Agreements and their relevance to the Digital Economy

The table below briefly covers the scope of each article under MLA to tackle BEPS strategies.

Article Reference	Nature of Article	Scope of Article	Relevance to India	Remarks
Article 2	Interpretation of treaties	Notifying treaties covered by MLI	India has notified 93 treaties but the treaty with China is yet to be notified	
Article 3	Fiscally transparent entities (FTEs)	MLI is intended to address the availability of benefits to entities that are fiscally transparent	India has reservations; hence India does not intend to provide treaty benefit to FTEs	As a practice, India does not follow the procedure of allowing treaty benefit to FTEs. However, for the US and the UK, the treaty has rules to determine whether benefits can be provided to LLPs
Article 4	Dual resident entities	This provision is intended to modify the tie-breaker test under treaties for persons other than individuals. The Competent Authorities of treaty partner countries shall determine the residential status of dual resident entities other than individuals based on POEM, and so on	India has opted to follow and has not made any reservetions. If other treaty partner countries express reservetions, India will not be able enforce this clause	Cyprus, Sweden, Luxembourg, Canada, and France have reservetions on this article; hence India will not be able to enforce this clause with these countries

Article Reference	Nature of Article	Scope of Article	Relevance to India	Remarks
Article 5	Methods to eliminate double taxation	Recommends three methods to eliminate double taxation	India chose option C — Credit method	
Article 6	Minimum standard	Expressly states that the purpose of the treaty is ***not to create opportunities for non-taxation or reduced taxation*** through tax evasion or avoidance	India follows the minimum standard	
Article 7	Prevention of treaty abuse	Provides the following approaches to curb treaty abuse: • Principal purpose test • A simplified limitation of benefits clause • A detailed limitation of benefits clause	India has opted for Principal Purpose Test and a simplified limitation of benefits clause	If India's treaty partners have decided not to apply this approach in their CTA, then India may not enforce this for them. Cyprus, the Netherlands, Singapore, Australia, Luxembourg, the United Kingdom, Japan, Ireland, France, Canada, and Sweden are not following the simplified limitation of benefits clause
Article 8	Dividend transfer	Introduces additional criteria of	India has notified this clause	Canada, Singapore, and

Article Reference	Nature of Article	Scope of Article	Relevance to India	Remarks
	transactions	"365 days minimum holding period" for the shareholder to avail concessional tax rates under CTA	as a part of CTA. However, this will apply to the India-Portugal treaty which has a two-year threshold	Denmark have expressed reservations on this article in their respective treaties. Hence India cannot enforce this clause with them
Article 9	Capital gains from alienation of shares or interest of entities deriving their value principally from immovable property	Introduces additional criteria of "365 days minimum holding period" in case of gains arising from alienation of shares or other participation rights if such shares or rights derive more than a specified percentage of their value from immovable property situated in the source jurisdiction. Optional provision of inserting a minimum value derivation criterion of 50 percent of their value directly or indirectly from immovable property	India has opted for minimum holding period threshold along with minimum value derivation criterion of 50 percent	Cyprus, Sweden, Canada, Singapore, Luxembourg, and the United Kingdom have expressed reservations in applying this article. Therefore, India cannot enforce this clause with these countries
Article 10	Anti-Abuse rule of PE	This article deals with a situation,	India has not made any re-	Cyprus, Sweden, Singapore,

Article Reference	Nature of Article	Scope of Article	Relevance to India	Remarks
	located in a third jurisdiction	where an enterprise of the country of residence derives income from the country of source, and such income is considered by the country of residence as being attributed to a PE of the enterprise in a third jurisdiction. If the profits attributable to the PE are exempt in the country of residence, the benefits of the CTA will not be available in respect of any income on which the tax in the third jurisdiction (i.e., where the PE is located) is less than 60% of the tax that would be imposable in the country of residence if the PE had been situated there	servations on the application of this article; hence its application depends on whether India's treaty partners express any reservations	Canada, the Netherlands, France, Australia, Ireland, Luxembourg, and the United Kingdom have expressed their right not to apply this article. Being a treaty partner, India cannot enforce this clause
Article 11	Application of tax agreements to restrict a	Preserves the right of jurisdiction to tax its own residents	India is silent on this article. Hence it is applicable to	

Article Reference	Nature of Article	Scope of Article	Relevance to India	Remarks
	party's right to tax its own residents		all the treaties notified unless the other country expresses reservations	
Article 12	Artificial avoidance of PE status through commissionaire arrangements and similar strategies	This article provides that a PE will include situations where: (a) a person acts on behalf of an enterprise and habitually concludes contracts, or habitually plays a principal role in the conclusion of contracts that are routinely concluded without material modification by the enterprise (b) These contracts are in the name of the enterprise or for transfer of ownership over goods owned by that enterprise or for provision of services by that enterprise	India has not made any reservations on this article. It is therefore applicable to all the treaties notified unless the other country expresses reservations	Cyprus, Sweden, Singapore, Canada, Australia, Ireland, Luxembourg, and the United Kingdom have expressed their right not to apply this article. Hence India being a treaty partner cannot enforce this clause

Article Reference	Nature of Article	Scope of Article	Relevance to India	Remarks
		(*The intention of this Article is to widen the scope of PE by removing exemptions to certain activities which were considered as preparatory and auxiliary services.*)		
Article 13	Artificial avoidance of PE status through specific activity exemptions	This article provides for two options regarding the scope of the specific activity exemptions contained in the definition of PE (i.e., a place of storage, display, processing, purchase of goods etc.). Under option A, the article is proposed to be modified to provide that the activities listed therein will be deemed not to constitute a PE only if they are of a preparatory or auxiliary character. Option B envisages that the specific activities	India has chosen to apply option A in its covered agreements. However, its applicability to India's treaties will depend on whether its treaty partners have also chosen the same option. In addition, India has chosen to apply the anti-fragmentation rule which will apply to a CTA only if the other CTA partner has chosen to apply the provision	Cyprus, Sweden, and Canada have chosen not to apply this article in their CTA. Hence India cannot enforce this clause with them. The Netherlands, Australia, and Japan have decided to apply option A; while France, Ireland, and Luxembourg have chosen to apply option B

Article Reference	Nature of Article	Scope of Article	Relevance to India	Remarks
		listed in the definition of PE are intrinsically preparatory or auxiliary and, in order to provide greater certainty for both tax administrations and taxpayers, takes the view that these activities should not be subject to the condition that they be of a preparatory or auxiliary character		
Article 14	Splitting up of contracts	BEPS Action point 7 identifies the issue of splitting up of contracts. The MLA specifies that activities relating to building site, construction or installation and connected activeties at the same site/project by closely related enterprises should be aggregated to determine if the threshold is satisfied	India has not expressed reservations to this article; its applicability is dependent on whether the other country has reservations as a part of its CTA	Cyprus, Sweden, Canada, Singapore, Luxembourg, Japan, and the United Kingdom have expressed their right not to apply this article. Hence India cannot enforce its application of with these countries

Article Reference	Nature of Article	Scope of Article	Relevance to India	Remarks
Article 15	Definition of a person in the context of Articles 12, 13 & 14	Article 15 provides that entities will be considered closely connected if one controls the other or both are under common control.	India has not expressed its reservations against this clause. Hence it will apply unless other countries express reservetions	
Article 16	Mutual Agreement Procedure (MAP)	Article 16 provides for mandatory inclusion of MAP provisions in CTA	India has reserved its right for not adopting the modified MLI provisions, as it will meet the minimum standard by allowing MAP access in the resident state and implementing bilateral notification or consultation process.	
Article 17	Requires jurisdictions to make appropriate corresponding adjustments in transfer pricing cases	India has chosen to apply the said provision except for CTAs where the provisions already exist		

Article Reference	Nature of Article	Scope of Article	Relevance to India	Remarks
Article 18 to 26	Mandatory binding arbitration	Part VI of the Multilateral Convention provides for mandatory binding arbitration in cases where competent authorities are unable to reach an agreement to resolve a case under the MAP	India has not opted for mandatory arbitration	

Impact of Multilateral Agreements on Taxation of Digital Economy

While the preceding table summarises the position of MLA and India's stand vis-à-vis respective countries, the pertinent issue is whether these multilateral agreements will significantly impact the digital economy. In India, section 9 of the Income-tax Act, 1961 has been amended by introducing explanation 2A expanding the scope of business connection to include Significant Economic Presence (SEP).

Explanation 2A to section 9(1)(i) of the Act defines SEP as:

> transaction in respect of any goods, services or property carried out by a non-resident in India, including the provision of download of data or software in India, if the aggregate of payments arising from such transaction or transactions during the previous year exceeds such amount as may be prescribed; or
>
> systematic and continuous soliciting of business activities or engaging in interaction with such number of users as may be prescribed in India through digital means.

The section further provides that the transactions or activities shall constitute significant economic presence in India, whether or not the agreement for such transactions or activities is entered into in India, or the non-resident has a residence or place of business in India or renders services in India. Further it is also provided that only so much of income as is attributable to the transactions or activities referred above shall be deemed to accrue or arise in India.[55]

Given the above definition, the activities of e-commerce companies can be brought under the purview of SEP. However, the definition of PE under the DTAA has not been modified yet. In the absence of corresponding provision under DTAA, the expanded scope will not have the desired impact as the provisions of DTAA or domestic tax law whichever is more beneficial shall be applicable.

Unless the DTAA is modified, the SEP may not be an effective tool in bringing revenue on digital transactions into the tax net.

Country-specific proposals on taxation of digital economy are summarised in Annexure 1.

55. Explanation 2A to Section 9(1)(i) of Income-tax Act 1961.

Chapter 5

OECD RECOMMENDATIONS ON PILLAR 1 & PILLAR 2 – OVERVIEW

Introduction

Lack of clarity on the definition and application of the concept of permanent establishment (PE) to digital economy models, adoption of sourcing approach, increased digital trend in business and the enhanced use of digital technology as a medium for conducting business are posing new challenges both for the taxation systems of countries to implement and exercise the taxing right and for e-commerce players .

A wide cross-section is of the view that the traditional concepts of PE, sourcing principle, and arm's length principle are no longer effective in guiding the development of taxation system for the digital economy, and thus lead to a significant loss of revenue.

In these circumstances, countries are looking to new approaches to tax revenue generated from the digital economy.

Outline of Pillar 1 and Pillar 2

The BEPS action point 1[56] identified the challenges on taxation of the digital economy. Consequently, the inclusive framework, comprising 137 members, issued *Tax Challenges arising from Digitalisation–Interim Report 2018*[57], recognising the need for a global solution.

The report identified that the following characteristics are prevalent in digital markets:

- Scale without mass
- Reliance on intangible assets

---

56. Action 1 Tax Challenges Arising from Digitalisation, OECD BEPS available at https://www.oecd.org/tax/beps/beps-actions/action1/; last viewed on July 07, 2021.
57. OECD (2018), *Tax Challenges Arising from Digitalisation – Interim Report 2018: Inclusive Framework on BEPS*, OECD/G20 Base Erosion and Profit Shifting Project, OECD Publishing, Paris, https://doi.org/10.1787/9789264293083-en; last viewed on July 07, 2021.

- Data and user participation

The report also notes two fundamental concepts relating to allocation of taxing rights between jurisdictions that must be reviewed:

- Nexus, i.e., the threshold to create taxable presence
- Profit allocation

Following the interim report findings, the inclusive framework agreed upon the outline of a "unified approach" architecture as the basis of negotiation of Pillar 1 solution.[58].

Pillar 1 Blueprint

Pillar 1 aims to modify the International Tax system so that it aligns with the new business models by making changes to the *Profit Allocation* and *Nexus* rules applicable to business profits. The fundamental shift in allocation of business profits is that it expands the taxing rights of market jurisdictions, i.e., location of users.

The key elements of Pillar 1 are grouped into three components:

- A new taxing right for market jurisdictions over a share of residual profit calculated at MNE[59] group level (Amount A)
- A fixed return for certain baseline marketing and distribution activities taking place physically in a market jurisdiction in line with Arm's Length Price (Amount B)
- Processes to improve tax certainty through effective dispute prevention and resolution mechanisms
- Eleven building blocks have been identified as essential to the construction of Pillar 1

58. – OECD (2020), *Tax Challenges Arising from Digitalisation – Report on Pillar One Blueprint: Inclusive Framework on BEPS*, OECD/G20 Base Erosion and Profit Shifting Project, Para 5 of Chapter 1 of Report on Pillar 1 Blueprint, OECD Publishing, Paris, https://doi.org/10.1787/beba0634-en, last viewed on July 07, 2021.

59. The term "MNE Group" means any Group that (i) includes two or more enterprises the tax residence for which is in different jurisdictions, or includes an enterprise that is resident for tax purposes in one jurisdiction and is subject to tax with respect to the business carried out through a permanent establishment in another jurisdiction, and (ii) is not an Excluded MNE Group. Available at: https://www.oecd.org/ctp/transfer-pricing/beps-action-13-country-by-country-reporting-implementation-package.pdf, p. 11.

Scope of Pillar 1

- The new taxing right established through Amount A applies to MNEs based on the Activity test and Threshold test.
- The two categories of activities in scope for the new taxing right through Amount A are (i) Automated digital services (ADS) and (ii) Consumer facing business.
- The definition of ADS comprises ADS activities, a negative list of non-ADS activities and general definition.

Positive List of Non-ADS activities	Negative List of Non-ADS activities
(i) Online advertising services	(i) Customised professional services
(ii) Sale or other alienation of user data	(ii) Online sale of goods and services other than ADS
(iii) Online search engine	(iii) Revenue from sale of physical goods irrespective of network connectivity
(iv) Social media platforms	(iv) Services providing access to the internet or another electronic network
(v) Online intermediation platforms	
(vi) Digital content services	
(vii) Online gaming	
(viii) Standardised online teaching services	
(ix) Cloud computing services	

- The general definition of ADS is structured on two key elements: (i) Automation (based on system and requires minimal human involvement to provide the service on the part of service provider) and (ii) Digital (provided over the internet or electronic network)

- The hierarchy for determining ADS is based on whether it falls under the positive or negative list. However, if an activity is not within the purview of the positive or negative list, then one needs to consider whether the business activity is covered under ADS.
- The Pillar 1 blueprint defines each category under the positive and negative list of services[60].
- The scope of Pillar 1 includes Consumer facing business (CFB).
- CFBs are defined as those businesses that generate revenues from the sale of goods and services of a type commonly sold to customers including those selling indirectly through intermediaries and by way of franchising and licensing.[61]
- CFB is (i) the MNE that is the owner of the consumer product/service and holder of the rights to the connected intangible property (including franchisors and licensors), i.e., the MNE whose "face" is apparent to the consumer and (ii) the MNE that is the "retailer" or other contractual counterparty of the consumer (if separate from the "owner"), as they have a direct relationship to the consumer (including franchisees and licensees that sell the consumer product directly). It does not include other third party MNEs, such as manufacturers, wholesalers and distributors, which have no relationship with the customer — whether contractual or otherwise.
- CFB covers not only direct selling but even sales through resellers/ intermediaries that perform routine tasks like minor assembly/ packaging.
- For this purpose, "consumer" means an individual (whether or not the direct purchaser) who acquires a good or service for personal purposes rather than for commercial or professional purposes.
- The CFB model includes sale of consumer goods and services through franchise arrangements or licensing arrangement instead of direct sale to customer.

---

60. OECD (2020), *Tax Challenges Arising from Digitalisation – Report on Pillar One Blueprint: Inclusive Framework on BEPS*, OECD/G20 Base Erosion and Profit Shifting Project. pp 23-35, OECD Publishing, Paris, https://doi.org/10.1787/beba0634-en, last viewed on July 07, 2021.

61 *Id* p. 21.

- The scope of CFB does not include (i) natural resources, (ii) construction, sale and leasing of residential property, (iii) financial services, and (iv) international airline and shipping business.

Threshold Test

- Considering the cost-benefit analysis, it is recognised that rules should not apply to MNEs below certain threshold limit for determining Amount A.
- Again, the same issue will apply for MNEs who may cross the threshold limit but have negligible foreign source income.
- Hence the threshold limit is determined on the basis of:
    - Global Revenue test
    - De-Minimis foreign in scope revenue test
- The threshold limit for Global Revenue test is kept at € 750 million (same as applicable for Country-by-Country Reporting. If an MNE's revenue is less than € 750 million, the rule is not applicable.

New Nexus Rules

- The nexus rule is intended to protect the interests of smaller jurisdictions and developing economies.
- The Threshold test scope seeks to capture MNEs that are able to participate in an active and sustained manner in the economic life of market jurisdictions through constant engagement.
- The nexus rules act differently for ADS and CFB.
- According to the blueprint, the nexus *for*
    - ADS is achieved if revenue is more than € X million a year.
    - CFB exists if revenue is more than € X million a year, along with a plus factor to indicate a sustained and significant engagement with the market.
- The smaller countries may fix country-specific sales.

- For CFB, the possible additional plus factors being examined by framework are
    - (i) Physical presence in the form of PE or the residence of a group entity,
    - (ii) Physical presence falls short of PE, and
    - (iii) Undertaking of sustained marketing, advertising and promotion activities to support in scope sales in the market jurisdiction.

Revenue Sourcing Rules[62]

- The revenue sourcing rules determine the revenue that would be treated as deriving from a particular market jurisdiction.
- These rules are relevant for applying scope rules, nexus rules, and Amount A formula.
- An MNE must apply the revenue sourcing rules that are relevant to each type(s) of revenue(s) it generates.
- An MNE will apply the indicator that appears first in the hierarchy of indicators, unless this
- Information is unavailable or unreliable as noted within each rule.
- Information is only considered unavailable if it is not within the MNE's possession after reasonable steps were taken to obtain the information but in vain.
- Information is considered unreliable if the MNE can justify that the indicator is not a true representation of the principle in the source rule.
- If an indicator is unavailable or unreliable, the MNE should seek to apply the next indicator in the hierarchy. In the event that all of the indicators in the hierarchy are unavailable (after having taken reasonable steps to obtain it) or unreliable, the MNE must apply the

---

62. OECD (2020), *Tax Challenges Arising from Digitalisation – Report on Pillar One Blueprint: Inclusive Framework on BEPS*, OECD/G20 Base Erosion and Profit Shifting Project, Chapter 4, OECD Publishing, Paris, https://doi.org/10.1787/beba0634-en, last viewed on July 07, 2021.

sourcing rule based on alternative available information and document the approach taken.

- An MNE must retain documentation as set out in these rules.
- The summary sourcing rules and indicators for different business are summarised in Annexure 2.

Tax Base Determinations

- Amount A is a new taxing right over a share of the residual profit of MNE groups that fall within its defined scope.
- The tax base is determined on the basis of the profits of a group instead of a separate entity basis, and it is necessary to start with consolidated group financial accounts.
- The Amount A tax base will be quantified using an adjusted Profit Before Tax (PBT) measure that will be derived from the consolidated financial accounts.
- The inclusive framework group has recommended that for ease of administration only a limited number of book-to-adjustments will apply to determine the relevant measure of PBT. The adjustments will include exclusion of income-tax expenses, exclusion of dividend income and gains or losses in connection with shares and expenses not deductible for corporate income tax as applicable in most jurisdictions.
- The group recognises the need for segmentation if the MNE has activity outside the scope.
- All MNE groups falling in the scope of Amount A would need to break down their revenue between ADS, CFB and out-of-scope activities, as may be required for the scope and nexus rules.
- Loss carry forward rules will apply through earn-out mechanism at the level of the group or segment.
- The losses generated over a given tax period under Amount A will not be allocated to market jurisdictions. They will be pooled in a single account for the relevant segment and carried forward to subsequent years. Due to this, no profit under Amount A would arise for that segment until historic losses reported in that account have been fully absorbed.

- This carry forward regime will be kept separate from any existing domestic loss carry-forward rules and include specific rules to deal with business reorganisations.

Profit Allocation

The new taxing right is based on a three-tier mechanism.

- Amount A

  Step 1

  - Determine the group's total profit
  - PBT as per consolidated financial statements
  - Consideration being given to the use of business line and or regional segmentation

  Step 2

  - Determine residual profit by excluding deemed routine profit
  - Fixed percentages
  - Possible variation by industry

  Step 3

  - Allocate a proportion of deemed residual profit attribution to market countries
  - Fixed percentages.
  - Possible variation by industry

  Step 4

  - Allocate profits between market countries using allocation keys

- Amount B

  - Establish a fixed return for "baseline" or routine marketing and distribution of activities

- Amount C

  - Additional return based on arm's length transfer pricing and recognising profit in excess of the return calculated under Amount B

- Provides the market and distribution activities taking place in the market country go beyond the baseline level of functionality, or the group or company performs other business activities in the county unrelated to marketing and distribution

Points for Consideration

- The blueprint for Pillar 1 has a significant impact on taxation of the digital economy, but the approach has multiple challenges both at conceptual and implementation levels.
- It is based on the premise that PE for digital business has arisen through digital presence, which may not be the real case.
- The definition of PE and preparatory and auxiliary activities need to undergo changes in the Multilateral Treaty; the existing definition of PE and exemption are not sufficient to capture the profits arising out of digital transactions.
- The theory of Pillar 1 and Pillar 2 makes the existing method of Attribution of Profits redundant.
- Attribution of Profits, based on the "Separate entity approach" will become redundant with the introduction of Pillar 1 and Pillar 2.
- Moreover, attribution of profits is skewed in favour of developing economies that can benefit from it only if they have a better negotiating and bargaining power.
- Historically, developed countries were not in favour of any attribution of profits which is skewed in favour of the PE country.
- The approach is also based on the "market based" theory which has a different connotation for different geographies, as it is based on the region's market, advertising spend, and customer reach.
- Profit attribution is also based on residual profit method for excess returns. Though the Profit Split Method (PSM) under Transfer Pricing is one of the recognised methods for tax calculation, it is not followed much because of the challenges in determining the base for residual profit and computation of residual profit. It is observed that the revenue authorities of different countries usually do not accept a common base for PSM.

- The approach also stems from the fact that every digital transaction creates revenue for the source country based on customer presence and market. The nexus theory for taxing digital economy is inappropriate as it will be challenging for both the companies and home countries.
- Considering the manner in which business is conducted through digital transactions, implementing the concept is fraught with challenges, as practical issues will arise on computation of base profit, allocation and residual profit.

Conclusion

It is debatable whether Pillar 1 and Pillar 2 will achieve the purpose of taxation of digital economy, as challenges exist both at the conceptual and implementation levels. It is therefore important to work out an alternative structure that is easier to understand and implement.[63]

63. This chapter is intended to give an overview of Pillar 1 and Pillar 2 and not critically analyse. We are working on a separate analysis identifying the challenges and suggesting an alternative structure.

Chapter 6

INTERNATIONAL CASE LAW

South Dakota v. Wayfair, Inc., et al.

Court: Supreme Court, United States

The *South Dakota v. Wayfair, Inc.*[64], case deals with applying alternate rule to the physical presence rule for out-of-state retailers who sell goods or services to the residents of the state, without having a physical presence.

Background/Facts

In the case at hand, the issue was whether an out-of-state seller without a physical presence in the state should be required to collect and remit the state's sales tax.

- South Dakota enacted a law requiring an out-of-state seller to collect and remit sales tax if the seller, on an annual basis, delivers goods or services with a value of more than USD 100,000 into the state, or engages in 200 or more separate transactions for the delivery of goods or services into the state.
- Under the Commerce Clause of the US Constitution, the US Supreme Court stipulates, as one of the conditions for US state sales taxes to be validly imposed, that the state sales taxes apply only to an activity with a substantial nexus with the taxing state.
- Based on the substantial nexus requirement, the US Supreme Court in its decision in the case of *Quill Corp.* v. *North Dakota*[65] affirmed that a US state could not ask a retailer to collect taxes if it did not have a physical presence in the state.
- The issue, therefore, was whether the decision in Quill was a controlling precedent. During the legal proceedings, the South Dakota State Supreme Court held the levy of sales tax under the state laws

64. 901 N.W.2d 754.
65. 504 U.S. 298 (1992).

was unconstitutional based on the physical presence rule of Quill. Subsequently, the tax authorities, South Dakota, appealed to the US Supreme Court.

Observations and Ruling of the US Supreme Court

As for the physical presence rule, the US Supreme Court observed that:

(i) the physical presence rule had been criticised for giving out-of-state sellers an advantage; moreover, each year the economic reality was less and less taken into account, resulting in significant revenue losses to the US states;

(ii) the physical presence rule was not necessary for interpreting the substantial nexus requirement, which is closely related to the due process requirement that there is some definite link, some minimum connection, between a state and the person, property or transaction it seeks to tax;

(iii) the physical presence rule created market distortions by providing a tax shelter for businesses that limit their physical presence in a state but sell their goods and services to the state's consumers online and offer incentives to avoid physical presence in multiple US states; and

(iv) the physical presence rule treated economically identical actors differently by giving online retailers an arbitrary advantage over their brick-and-mortar competitors who collected state sales taxes. E.g., a small business that maintained a few items of inventory in a warehouse is subject to sales tax due to its physical presence, while an online seller, with a pervasive internet presence, was not taxed for the sale of the same items.

- The US Supreme Court also observed that the physical presence stipulation, as set out in the Quill case, did not align with modern e-commerce paradigms; thus, it was an extraordinary imposition by the judiciary on states' authority to collect taxes and perform critical public functions.
- The US Supreme Court further stated that the principle of 'stare decisis' no longer supports the physical presence rule because the internet's prevalence and power have disrupted the dynamics of the national economy.

- After deciding to remove the physical presence rule from the substantial nexus requirement, the US Supreme Court held that the South Dakota Act sufficiently satisfied the substantial nexus requirement, because the Act applies only to sellers that engage in a significant number of transactions in the state (i.e., annual sales with a value of more than USD 100,000 or at least 200 separate transactions). The US Supreme Court noted that the persons subject to the tax in this case were all large national companies that undoubtedly maintained an extensive virtual presence in South Dakota.
- The US Supreme Court further noted that other principles of the Commerce Clause doctrine might invalidate the Act, but these principles were not litigated or briefed, so it did not need to resolve them at the present time.
- The US Supreme Court also noted that South Dakota's tax system includes several features that prevent discrimination against, or undue burdens upon, interstate commerce: (1) the Act applies a safe harbour to those who transact only limited business in South Dakota; (2) the Act ensures that no obligation to remit the sales tax may be applied retroactively; (3) South Dakota is one of more than 20 US states that have adopted the Streamlined Sales and Use Tax agreement, to standardise taxes and reduce administrative and compliance costs (i.e., it requires a single, state-level tax administration, uniform definitions of products and services, simplified tax rate structures, and other uniform rules); and (4) it provides sellers access to sales tax administration software paid for by the state, and sellers who choose to use the software are immune from audit liability.
- Based on the above observations, the US Supreme Court vacated the decision of the South Dakota State Supreme Court and remanded the case for further proceedings.

Conclusion

The US Supreme Court nullified the requirement of physical presence for an enterprise to be taxable if there were other factors to prove substantial nexus for taxation.

The case was decided by a five-four majority of the nine US Supreme Court Justices. The four dissenting Justices opined that the US Congress, and not the Court, should decide whether to depart from the physical presence rule as it involves an important question on the current economic policy.

Dell Products Ltd (DPL) v. General State Administration (2016, 2015)

Court: Supreme Court of Spain

This case[66] deals with the concept of fixed place permanent establishment (PE) wherein the term 'availability' was explained by the Supreme Court of Spain. It observed that the conventional definition of PE does not hold good in the digital economy where 'virtual economic presence' is a key factor. This case also laid down the parameters for evaluating a dependent agent PE.

Background/Facts

DESA, a wholly owned subsidiary of Dell Products Ltd (DPL), and its staff carried out a host of activities in Spain, relating to DPL's products such as advertising and marketing, sale and distribution, order management, control of receipts, and collection management for all DPL's customers in the country. It also performed warehouse and logistics services, installation services, collection management, solvency and credit control. Spain's Revenue authorities assessed DPL for tax on profits attributable to DESA's activities on the grounds that DESA constituted a 'permanent establishment' of DPL.

Observations of Lower Courts

Fixed place PE

- The concept of fixed place PE includes any premises or facilities used to carry out an enterprise's economic activity whether or not it is used exclusively for the purpose, and regardless of the title under which such use is made. In order to be a fixed PE, there must be a certain degree of permanence in time in the state's territory, and activities carried out in the premises must be those of the enterprise.
- DESA's facilities were available to DPL for its activities carried out through DESA's staff, but the activities themselves constituted the core of DPL's corporate aim.

66. STS 2861/2016.

- Further, DESA's activities were more than mere storage services, which are excluded from PE, and were not of an ancillary character either. Therefore, DESA constituted a fixed place PE of DPL.

Dependent agent PE

- Based on the commercial agency agreement, DESA followed DPL's instructions for authorising prices and commissions, accepting or rejecting requests for delivery, and even submitted periodic reports to DPL. Moreover, DPL had the right to inspect DESA's records and premises, authorise purchase of products, and had control over the intellectual property rights.
- These activities prove that DESA was not an independent agent but a dependent agent PE of DPL.

Arguments of the Assessee

Fixed place PE

- The premises considered as the fixed place of business was never available to the assessee. It deems the term 'availability' to refer only to actual availability, i.e., availability of facilities obtained through the owner's consent or person in possession thereof for their use. The concept of 'availability' implies a direct relationship between the available facility and the non-resident entity and not an indirect one as pointed out by the lower authorities, because a different clause relating to dependent agents is applicable in that case.
- As per OECD's interpretation, the term 'availability' must be interpreted as the physical use of the establishment by the non-resident entity and not its use under supervision. For DESA's facilities to be considered as 'available' to DPL and to constitute a fixed place of business, DPL should have regularly exercised the right to use them; this fact has not been proven at any court level.
- Further, it is not only necessary that a fixed place exists but also that business activity must be carried out through it. This is called the "functional aspect of the PE". DPL asserted that it carried out the activities constituting its corporate aim from Ireland and that it had

sufficient staff to carry out all its activities in Spain. Thus, there was either no involvement or only ancillary involvement of DESA.

Dependent agent PE

- DPL argued that in terms of Article 5(5) of the Ireland-Spain tax treaty, "conclude contracts in the name of the enterprise" refers to the bond between the third party and the principal, which does not arise in commercial agency agreements, where the agent acts in its own name and not in that of the principal. It necessarily requires the non-resident to be bound by the operations carried out by the agent and be a contracting entity to third parties. The lower authorities have taken a few clauses of the commercial agency agreement between DPL and DESA out of context and ignored that DESA is a legally and financially independent agent, acting in the ordinary course of its business.
- DESA not only assumes the risk of local sales but also supports its own business risk. Merely belonging to the same group does not render DESA financially dependent; local sales are in DESA's name and on its own behalf. Besides, DESA will continue to carry out its business even if it loses the DPL account. The practice of updating DPL and rendering accounts is like any customer-supplier service relationship. DESA is completely free to set sale prices both within the agreed range and above it. DESA decides on the approval or rejection of orders/transactions at prices other than those suggested by DPL. DESA also does not acquire product ownership but only sells it.
- Activities carried out by DESA are not absolutely fundamental for DPL, as DPL's corporate aim is marketing and distribution of Dell products whereas DESA's main activity is brokering of sales.

Spain's Supreme Court Ruling

Fixed place PE

- The term 'availability' means the use of fixed place of business by the non-resident through another entity who carried out the activities on DPL's request and are under its control, and such activities are part of its core corporate aim. This could be referred to as a mediate use but one which serves the same aim and purpose as a direct use by the non-resident's staff. The scope of 'availability' of the place is based on the premise that the same business activities as those of the non-resident enterprise must be carried out there.

- According to OECD's commentary, the term 'place of business' includes any premises, facilities or material means used to carry out the enterprise's activities whether or not they are exclusively for that purpose. It could be a specific space available to conduct business even if there is no official premises, as there is no requirement of a formal legal title to use it. The word 'through' must be understood in its broadest sense to include business activities carried out at a specific space available to the enterprise for that purpose. Therefore, there is a high degree of flexibility given to the term 'fixed place of business' to include another enterprise's facilities.
- Essentially, 'availability' includes "acting on behalf of the enterprise". The function and the purpose of the convention are to regulate aspects of international taxation. The new business environment in digital world and commercial globalisation require interpretation of the applicable laws adapted to this new reality, in which it is essential to address the substance of the new business activity models. It thus cannot be inferred that there is a requirement for a direct relationship and physical use of the establishment.
- Further, it is irrelevant whether the non-resident carries on business in Ireland or not, whether the number of people working in Spain is small or large, as well as the fact that DPL assumes the risk of bad debts. Without prejudice to the activities carried out by DPL in Ireland, the substantial nature of the business activities/functions carried out by DPL through DESA's facilities and its staff have been established, proving that DESA is not acting as a mere ancillary body of DPL. These facts are deemed to have been proven in the lower courts. Therefore, DESA constitutes a fixed place PE of DPL.

Dependent agent PE

- In order to hold a PE, the Ireland-Spain tax treaty requires the person to be acting on behalf of an enterprise, and interpreting that "acting on behalf of the enterprise" necessarily requires direct representation would be going beyond the wording of the provision and does not follow from the application of the interpretation criteria. The phrase 'on behalf of' must be understood to refer to the power the commission agents need to have in order to bind the principal to the contract concluded, even if this does not give rise to a legal relationship between the principal and the contracting third party.

- DESA followed DPL's instructions. DPL authorised purchase of products, prices and commissions and accepted or rejected requests for delivery. Besides, DESA submitted periodic reports to DPL that had the right to inspect DESA's records and premises, along with control over intellectual property rights. Considering these circumstances, a 'relationship of dependence' exists between DPL and DESA. A commission agent acting in its name on behalf of another must be considered a dependent agent. What must be looked into is whether the agent has sufficient authority to bind the non-resident. In view of DPL's extensive powers of supervision and direction, DESA could not be said to operate as an independent agent.
- Moreover, organisational dependency exists between the companies, as they belong to the same parent company. DESA's intervention is, therefore, essential for marketing and distributing Dell products, which is DPL's corporate aim.
- In today's digital era, what determines an independent agent's financial and operational identity is not the way of formalising the contractual relationship but its existing functional and factual relationship, which must be ascertained based on all the circumstances surrounding the conduct of its business. Therefore, there is no room for a strict formalist-literal and static interpretation.

Conclusion

Spain's Supreme Court ruled that DESA constituted DPL's fixed place PE even though DPL had no physical/direct presence in the country. The ruling was based on the premise that DESA's facilities and staff carried out activities forming the core of DPL's corporate aim.

The Court also ruled out the static and literal interpretation of Article 5 of the Tax Treaties by taking into account the reality of global markets where multinational companies try to shift their profits to States with low taxation.

Further, the Supreme Court ruled that DPL had a dependent agent PE in Spain, considering the functional and factual circumstances; and it concluded that a relationship of dependence existed between DPL and DESA, irrespective of the contractual relationship. This view differs from courts in France and Norway, which have found that commissionaire arrangements do not give rise to a PE. Further, the OECD-BEPS initiative realised the need to reword Article 5 to cover such arrangements within the definition of PE, which suggests that the current treaties do not cover it.

Google India (P.) Ltd v. ACIT (2017)

Court: Income-tax Appellate Tribunal, India

This case[67] deals with the taxability of payments made for online advertising related services/facilities by Google India to Google Ireland.

Background/Facts

- Google India Private Limited (Google India) is a wholly owned subsidiary of Google International LLC, US. Google India had been appointed by Google Ireland Ltd (GIL) as a non-exclusive authorised distributor of 'Google Adwords' (now Google Ads) to advertisers in India.
- Under the Google Adwords Program Distribution Agreement, Google India was granted the marketing and distribution rights along with customer support services to the Adwords Program in India.
- During the financial year 2007-08 (relevant to assessment year 2008-09), Google India paid a distribution fee of ₹119 crore to GIL towards distribution rights granted under the agreement, without deducting tax at source under section 195 of the Income-tax Act, 1961 (the Act).
- For not deducting tax at source, Google India contended that since it is merely a reseller of advertisement space and is only performing marketing-related activities to promote the sale of advertisement space in India, the amount payable by it to GIL was advertisement fee, and not in the nature of royalty under the Act. Besides, it stated that the server on which Adwords resides is located outside India and

67. 2017 SCC OnLine ITAT 5941.

Google India has no control over it. Consequently, neither Google India nor the advertisers have any right to use or exploit the underlying intellectual property and software.

- However, the Assessing Officer (AO) held that the distribution rights are in the nature of intellectual property rights covered by similar property under the definition of royalty as per section 9(1)(vi) of the Act. The AO treated the distribution fee in the nature of royalty under the India-Ireland Double Taxation Avoidance Agreement (DTAA), being, among others, payment for the use of a secret process. Accordingly, the AO held that the distribution fee paid to GIL was subject to withholding tax in India under section 195 of the Act.
- The AO treated Google India as an 'assessee in default' according to section 201(1) for not deducting tax at source when the amount(s) in question were taxable in India.
- Aggrieved with the AO's order, Google India appealed before the Commissioner of Income-tax (Appeals) [CIT(A)], which too upheld the AO's order.

Observations and Ruling of the Tribunal

Whether payment made by Google India to GIL is taxable in India?

The Tribunal ruled in favour of the Revenue authorities and held that the payment made by Google India was in the nature of royalty. While doing so, the Tribunal inter alia observed as under:

- The Adwords Program Distribution Agreement allows Google India to access all intellectual property and confidential information used for activities related to the distribution agreement.
- For the purpose of marketing and distributing the Adwords Program, Google India is given the right to use GIL's valuable business asset, i.e., intellectual property in products and services.
- As Google India, through its search engine, has access to users' personal data such as name, age, gender, city and country of residence, as well as the IP address of the desktop/laptop/tablet along with their habits and other preferences, it is able to achieve successful audience targeting in online ads.

- Thus, the distribution agreement between Google India and GIL is not merely an agreement to provide advertisement space but also an agreement to focus advertisement to the intended customer.
- Further, the intellectual property of Google vests in the search engine, technology, associated software and other features; hence, the use of these tools for performing various activities, including accepting advertisements and providing before/after sales services, clearly falls within the ambit of royalty.
- The Tribunal further observed that even though Google India claimed to be earning revenue from the information technology enabled services (ITeS) segment under a separate outsourcing service agreement with GIL, inputs from ITeS are always required in the business model of Google India, without which there cannot be any targeted marketing for advertisements and promotion of sales of advertisers.
- Therefore, the services rendered under the ITeS agreement and the activities undertaken under the distribution agreement are inter-connected. Under the Distribution Agreement, Google India was duty bound to render various ITeS services and the Adwords program was one of the services provided under the ITeS agreement. This is only a mechanism/structure prepared by GIL to avoid payment of taxes.
- The Tribunal, however, noted that GIL had devised this mechanism/structure to avoid payment of taxes. Besides, Google India was permitted to use the trade name, trademarks, service marks, domains and other distinctive brand features of GIL solely under the Distribution Agreement on a non-exclusive, non-sub-licensable basis for the purposes of marketing and distribution of the Adwords program.
- Accordingly, it was held that the payments made by Google India under the agreement were not only for marketing and promoting Adwords but also for using Google brand features.
- Hence, the Tribunal concluded that Google India used Google brand features as a marketing tool for promoting and advertising, which is the main activity of Google India. Hence, even on this count, the

payment falls under the definition of royalty under the Act as well as the DTAA.

Whether withholding tax provisions are to be applied on receipt basis, considering that the payment made to GIL is chargeable in the hands of GIL on receipt basis under the India-Ireland DTAA?

- The argument of applying withholding tax provisions based on taxability in the hands of the recipient on a receipt basis under the India-Ireland DTAA was rejected by the Tribunal which observed that the benefit under the DTAA is available to a non-resident and not to a resident payer.
- It further held that GIL follows the mercantile system of accounting; hence, chargeability of the income would be in the year in which it is accrued and not in the year in which it is received.
- The Tribunal noted that the DTAA can only provide characterisation of the income, the country where it is to be paid, and the rate of tax. It is not within the scope of the DTAA to provide when the income is required to be charged to tax.
- The Tribunal also held that the literal rule of interpretation, which allows unscrupulous persons to misuse the provisions to avoid taxes, is not required to be followed when it defeats the intent of the provision.

Whether it is obligatory to approach the AO for determining taxability under Section 195 of the Act?

- The Tribunal observed that in terms of section 195 of the Act, Google India is obliged to deduct tax if it makes payment to a non-resident.
- The necessary safeguards under the Act, in the form of section 195(2), provide that in case an assessee is doubtful about the chargeability of an income to tax, it can apply to the AO to determine the chargeability of a sum to tax.
- In this case, no such application was made; hence, Google India was duty bound to deduct tax.

Validity of the proceedings under section 201 of the Act

- In so far as initiating proceedings under section 201(1A) is concerned, the Tribunal turned down Google India's challenge on initiating proceedings beyond a four-year period, in view of the Allahabad High Court's ruling in the case of *Mass Awash P. Ltd* v. *CIT,* (Int. Tax.) (2017). The court had held that the amended law under section 201, which requires initiation of proceedings within six years for a resident, would also be applicable in the case of a non-resident. The law provides for non-discrimination between a non-resident and a resident and requires equal treatment for both under the DTAA.

Conclusion

The ITAT held that the transaction was a design or structure prepared to avoid payment of taxes by the taxpayer.

Based on the terms and conditions of the agreement, the Tribunal held that the payment towards distribution rights is in the nature of royalty under the Act as well as under the DTAA because of the right to access not only technology but also customer data and intellectual property rights.

Google Ireland Ltd (2017)

Court: Administrative Court, France

The facts of this case are similar to those of the above case relating to Adwords program. However, the issue in this case pertains to 'permanent establishment' and not 'royalty'. It is interesting to note how courts of different nations are looking at the arrangement of Adwords program for taxation purpose.

Background/Facts

- The Google group inter alia provides an online advertisement service/platform called Adwords (now Google Ads), which is run by Google Ireland. In the Adwords system keywords (a word used to find information when researching) play a large role in determining the webpages where the advertising copy is to be displayed for viewing. Advertisers pay when web users click on the advertising copy. The contract signed between Google and the advertiser determines the maximum cost per click that the advertiser will assume, as multiple advertisers may select the same keywords. The maximum cost per click assumed by an advertiser contributes to determining the order in which the advertisement will appear on a web user's screen.

- Adwords services are generally provided in two modalities: First, online sales organisation (OLO) allows clients to independently manage their online advertisement activities; and the other, direct sales organisation (DSO) offers additional commercial assistance and account management services relating to a client's advertisement activities.
- A Marketing and Services Agreement (the Agreement) was signed on May 16, 2002 between Google France, a legal entity resident in France, and its parent company, Google Incorporated (Google USA). On July 1, 2004, the Agreement was ceded by Google USA to Google Ireland, another subsidiary.
- Pursuant to the Agreement, Google France performed certain activities relating to the Adwords programme for Google Ireland which remunerated Google France on a cost-plus basis with a profit mark-up of 8%.
- Under the terms of the Agreement, Google France agreed to provide "all services of assistance and advice required by Google Ireland for the purpose of the marketing and sale of online services provided in France"; these services included "marketing and demonstration of Google's online services"; and Google France also "contributed to market analysis and strategic analysis, including analysis of potential clients to whom online services could be sold".
- The French tax authorities contended that although the terms of the Agreement did not provide for concluding, signing or negotiating of contracts, Google France's employees were de facto vested with the power to sign contracts in the name of Google Ireland. The employees were engaged in both discussions with and taking of orders by advertisers, as well as aftersales and invoicing services.
- From the documents scrutinised during tax audit, the tax authorities opined that some employees of Google France were assigned the job of bringing in new clients in order to increase the company's

turnover. Even the internal communication records revealed that employees were engaged in managing client portfolios and negotiating contracts with clients. It appears that Google France hired an in-house lawyer to advice on negotiation and drafting of commercial contracts with clients in France and elsewhere in Europe. Further, Google France figured in many documents obtained by the tax authorities as "the seller" or as "responsible for the sales".

- Based on the above findings, the French tax authorities argued that Google Ireland carries out professional activity in France, namely the sale of online advertisement space through Google France; and hence concluded that Google France constitutes an agency permanent establishment (PE) of Google Ireland in France within the meaning of Article 2(9)(c) of the France-Ireland Tax Treaty (the Treaty).
- Pursuant to the above, the French tax authorities had issued a corrective assessment to Google Ireland Limited (Google Ireland) for the applicable tax years and subjected it to:
  - Corporate income tax and penalties in relation to PE and additional enterprise turnover tax
  - Withholding tax and penalties due on the royalties paid by Google Ireland to Google Netherlands to the extent these royalties related to the activities performed by the French PE of Google Ireland
  - Value added tax (VAT) on the advertisement services rendered by Google Ireland in France by means of the "fixed base" (FB) it disposed of in France for VAT purposes

Issues

- Whether Google Ireland had a PE in France at Google France's premises to carry out Adwords activities in the country under Articles 4 and 2(9)(c) of the Treaty and French law.
- Whether Google Ireland should pay French corporate income tax, additional enterprise turnover tax, withholding tax on royalties paid to Google Ireland's parent company for the profits realised by the PE, and French VAT on advertisement services provided via the PE.

Observations and the ruling of the Administrative Court (the Court)

Corporate income tax on account of PE and withholding tax on royalty payments:

The Court observed, under Articles 4 and 2(9) of the Treaty, that Google France could only constitute a PE of Google Ireland because the former acted as an agent, not independently while habitually exercising its authority to engage Google Ireland in commercial relations that relate to Google Ireland's activities in France.

- The obligations conferred on Google France in the Marketing and Services Agreement indicate that Google France was not independent of Google Ireland, even though Google Ireland was not directly controlling Google France. The cost-plus pricing arrangement between the entities was such that Google France did not carry any of the financial risks connected to its activities. Based on this, the Court rejected Google Ireland's argument that Google France was an agent with 'independent status' in terms of Article 2(9)(c) of the treaty.
- On the question whether Google France was a dependent agent of Google Ireland and whether it had the power to engage Google Ireland in commercial relations with its Adwords clients, the Court observed that the Agreement expressly provided as under:

  > "...during the provision of the assistance to the sale of the services, Google France agrees that it does not have the power to bind Google Ireland, nor to act as its mandatory or authorised representative mandated to acting for the account or in the name of Google Ireland or to sign contracts in the name of the latter. More specifically, Google France will not negotiate service or licence contracts for the account of Google Ireland nor will it accept such orders."
- Considering the above, the Court observed that even if certain activities performed by Google France's employees went beyond those conferred in the Agreement with Google Ireland, the tax authorities provided no evidence suggesting that these employees were mandated to act for the account and in the name of Google Ireland.

- The Court observed that the actual contracts did not disclose any evidence of Google France being mandated to sign contracts in the name of Google Ireland. The fact that Google France had agreed to out-of-court settlements with clients to end legal actions brought against it for liability or breach of contract, obliging these clients to waive any action against Google France "or any other company of the Google group", did not provide evidence that Google Ireland had delegated authority to Google France. Similarly, the fact that the (lower) civil courts had held in several decisions that Google France's liability exceeded the rendering of services under the Agreement did not imply that Google France acted for and in the name of Google Ireland.
- Further, the Court observed that in several Adwords contracts Google France's name was mentioned in its capacity as "sales rep" or "account manager", and this did not detract from the fact that the contracts were actually signed between the client and Google Ireland was the other contracting party.
- Even if the contracts were negotiated by employees of Google France, they had to be validated by Google Ireland before taking effect. Even if this validation process was purely formal and merely entailed an electronic signature by Google Ireland, it was held sufficient to condition the legal effect of the contracts.
- The Court rejected the tax authorities' claim that Google Ireland was legally and systematically bound by the contracts negotiated by the employees of Google France, as well as the claim that the Google Ireland determined the price of the Adwords service; the price was effectively determined by the numbers of clicks an advertisement received once it went online.
- The Court observed that Google France did not have the authority to conclude contracts in the name of Google Ireland, even if it could be considered to be a dependent agent of the latter. The Court thus held that the tax authorities had wrongly held Google France to be a PE of Google Ireland for the purpose of Article 2(9)(c) of the treaty.
- Accordingly, the Administrative Court held that the tax authorities had erred by levying corporate tax, as well as withholding tax on the royalty payments.

Additional enterprise turnover tax

- This is due by enterprises habitually exercising professional activities in France. The taxable base comprises the value of the immovable property that the taxpayer has at its disposal to perform its professional activities.
- The Court observed that it could not be derived from the Agreement signed between Google France and Google Ireland that the latter disposed of immovable property other than the properties at the disposal of Google France to perform its own activities mentioned in the Agreement.
- The tax authorities argued that in a premises of Google France in Paris several switch routers and other highly valued information and communications technology (ICT) equipment was found and Google France therefore provided Google Ireland with secured rooms, and surveillance and maintenance services vis-à-vis the ICT equipment in France.
- The Court, however, observed that Google Ireland provided legal statements, revealing the servers that hosted the "google.fr" website were located in the United States, and neither the Google search engine nor the ITC platform supporting it was situated in France. Switch routers and other ICT equipment in France merely had an auxiliary function, namely to facilitate quick access to the Google network, hosted on servers outside France. Also, the surveillance and maintenance services provided by Google France served to streamline data transfers and were not related to the performance of any activities in France.
- Based on these finds, the Administrative Court held that Google Ireland did not maintain immovable assets in France in the disputed tax years and, as such, the tax authorities had erred by imposing this tax.

Value Added Tax

- The Court observed that the place in which services were provided was deemed to be situated in France if the service provided had its seat of activities or a fixed base in France from which the services were rendered. The Court referred to the relevant jurisprudence of the European Court of Justice (ECJ) (Berkholz, July 4, 1985, C-168/84; and AR O Lease BV, July 17, 1997, C-190/95) and observed that a fixed place required a sufficient degree of permanence and suitable technical and human infrastructure to provide the services in an autonomous way.

- The Court observed, based on the facts described above, it was clear that Google Ireland did not dispose of sufficient technical equipment to render the advertisement services in an autonomous manner; thus, it did not dispose of a fixed base in France for VAT purposes. On these grounds, the Court held that the tax authorities had erred by submitting Google Ireland to VAT on the advertisement services provided in France before January 1, 2010, covered by the old "place of supplier" regime.
- For services provided as of January 1, 2010, falling under the new 'place of customer' regime, the Court observed the new rules provided that if the services were rendered by a VAT subject that was not established in France to customers in France, the customer was due to pay the tax. Because Google Ireland was not established in France, the Court held that the tax administration had erred by subjecting the company to French VAT for its activities in France.

Conclusion

The French Administrative Court majorly relied on the agreement and its terms to conclude that Google France did not form an agency PE of Google Ireland, as it was not mandated to act for the account and in the name of Google Ireland. It is worthwhile to note that in a similar arrangement between Google India and Google Ireland with regard to the 'Adwords programme', the Indian Income-tax Appellate Tribunal held the payments made to Google Ireland as "royalty" based on its observation that the terms of the Agreement allowed Google India access to intellectual property rights of Google Ireland.

However, in the case of Valueclick International Ltd, involving similar facts and issues as presented in the Google France and Google Ireland case, the Supreme Administrative Court, France, made similar observations but ruled, on March 01, 2018, that Valueclick France does form a PE of Valueclick Ireland.

Earlier, in the case of Comala Defense — a Luxembourg-based company — that had obtained, developed, and subsequently sold a French immovable property asset, the Administrative Supreme Court held that Comala Defense formed a PE in France at the premises of a (indirectly related) French company that it had hired to perform all management aspects of the immovable property project.

In a press release of July 12, 2017, the French Government said it was analysing the Administrative Court's decisions, which were significant representations of the issue of taxing a fair share of profits realised by the digital economy in France.

CUB Pty Ltd v. Union of India and Ors (2008)

Court: Authority for Advance Rulings, India

This case[68] deals with the taxability of gains arising on transfer of intellectual property rights/intangible rights in the context of Indian laws vis-à-vis international principles.

Background/Facts

- The petitioner — CUB Pty Ltd., formerly known as Foster's Australia Ltd. or Foster's Group Ltd. — had a 100% subsidiary called Dismin India Private Ltd. (Dismin). Dismin held 100% shares of FBG India Holdings Ltd, Mauritius (FBG) which, in turn, held 100% shares of Foster's India Ltd. (Foster's India), which was incorporated on September 29, 1995.
- On October 13, 1997, a brand licence agreement (BLA) was executed between the petitioner, Foster's Group Ltd., and Foster's India. By virtue of the BLA, Foster's India was licensed to use in India four of the trademarks owned by the petitioner. In other words, the licensed trademarks continued to remain the absolute property of the petitioner. Foster's India was only permitted to use them in India as a licensee. In consideration of this licence, the petitioner received royalty and was subjected to withholding tax in India.

68. [2016] 383 ITR 617 (Del).

- On August 04, 2006, an agreement known as 'India sale purchase agreement' (ISPA) was executed in Melbourne between the petitioner, Foster's Group Ltd.; SABMiller (A & A2) Ltd. (hereinafter referred to as SABMiller); and SABMiller Africa & Asia B.V. Under the agreement, Dismin would sell the FBG shares to SABMiller; and the petitioner would sell its trademarks, including the four licensed trademarks Foster's India was allowed to use, as well as Foster's Brand Intellectual Property and grant of licence in relation to Foster's Brewing-related intellectual property, confined to India, to SABMiller.
- Following the ISPA, SABMiller became the owner of FBG, and hence, the owner of Foster's India and the 16 trademarks (including the four licensed trademarks) which were sold/assigned to SABMiller and its nominee, Skol Breweries Ltd.
- Under ISPA, before completing the sale and purchase of shares, the trademarks, Foster's Brand IP and the licence of Foster's Brewing IP were required to be terminated.
- On September 12, 2006, a deed of termination of the BLA was executed in Australia; and on the same day, a deed of assignment was executed in Australia, through which the petitioner assigned the 16 trademarks to Skol Breweries Ltd.
- Thereafter, the petitioner moved an application before the Authority for Advance Rulings (AAR) under section 245-Q of the Income-tax Act, 1961, seeking an advance ruling on, inter alia, the following question.

Question before the AAR

Whether the receipt arising to the applicant, from the transfer of its right, title and interest in and to the trademarks, Foster's Brand Intellectual Property and grant of exclusive perpetual licence of Foster Brewing Intellectual Property, is taxable in India, having regard to the provisions of the Income-tax Act, 1961, and the DTAA agreement between India and Australia?

AAR Held

The income arising from the transfer transaction of the trademarks is to be deemed income accruing in India on the basis of AAR's finding that the said IP rights were capital assets situated in India. However, income attributable to the grant of licence in relation to Foster's Brewing IP is not liable to be taxed under the Income-tax Act, 1961.

Aggrieved by AAR's ruling, the petitioner filed a petition before the High Court of Delhi.

Before High Court of Delhi

Arguments by the Petitioner

- The Foster's mark originated in Australia and the petitioner, an Australian company, was the owner of the brand/mark. The petitioner has granted licences to use the trademarks in various countries across the world (approximately between 70–100 countries), including in India.
- Pursuant to the grant of licence under the BLA, there was no shift in the situs (location or place) of the trademarks to India, since there was no transfer of any proprietary right. A licence to use a trademark confers only a limited right for the use of the mark and does not involve assignment of any proprietary interest therein. Since the trademarks were originally adopted by the petitioner in Australia, the intellectual property rights therein vested in the petitioner and the situs of those rights was Australia.
- The rights in a trademark are of common law origin and are protected thereunder. A trademark does not derive its existence from any statute and is protected even in the absence thereof. The registration of trademarks in India did not imply the migration of the intellectual property rights to India. Registration of a trademark only recognises a right that pre-exists in the trademark.
- The trademark's location is governed by the common law maxim, '*mobilia sequuntur personam*', which means the personal property held by a person is governed by the same laws that govern that person (the law of his domicile). This principle has been applied to determine the situs of intangible assets, which are to be determined by the situs of its owner. The principle behind this doctrine is that intangibles are subject to the immediate control of the owner and since intangibles do not have any real situs, the owner's domicile is the nearest approximation to their location.

- Since Indian law does not specifically provide for the situs of trademarks, the common law rule of '*mobilia sequuntur personam*' would be applicable.

Arguments by the tax department

The tax department, relying on AAR's decision, raised the following contentions:

- The trademarks — registered in India — along with the other aspects of the Foster's brand were nurtured in the country and had generated appreciable goodwill in the Indian market. When the petitioner sold the trademark and brand intellectual property rights for the territory of India, it received substantial proceeds for these intellectual property assets from SABMiller. The income accruing to the petitioner in respect of the transfer of capital assets situated in India was liable to tax in India.
- Even the fact that some of the trademarks were used elsewhere could not be used to deny their existence in India, as the intellectual property belonging to the petitioner had a 'tangible presence' in India at the time of the transfer. The registration of the trademarks also pointed to the roots these intellectual property assets had taken and the recognition they had gained in the country.
- The transfer of intellectual property rights, covered by the petition, was only in respect of India-specific intellectual property rights, but the mere fact that the transfer agreement occurred outside India did not render any income arising from the transactions non-taxable in India.
- The maxim of '*mobilia sequuntur personam*' would not apply in the present case. As these are business intangibles, their situs is effectively where the business is carried out and where the intangibles are protected under the local law. The trademarks and other IP rights, to the extent they related to India, would have to be deemed to be located in India and it did not matter as to where the owner was located.

Decision of the High Court

The High Court observed:

- An intangible capital asset, by its very nature, does not have any physical form. Therefore, it does not exist in a physical form at any particular location.
- The legislature could have provided for the location of an intangible capital asset, such as intellectual property rights, but it has not done so far as India is concerned. Where the legislature specifically wanted to provide for a particular situation, as in the case of shares — which, directly or indirectly, derive their value substantially from assets located in India — it did so. There is no such provision with regard to intangible assets, such as trademarks, brands, logos, etc. Therefore, the well-accepted principle of '*mobilia sequuntur personam*' would apply.
- The situs of an intangible asset's owner would be the closest approximation of the situs of the intangible asset. This is an internationally accepted rule, unless it is altered by local legislation. Since there is no such alteration in the Indian context, the situs of the trademarks and intellectual property rights, which were assigned pursuant to the ISPA, would not be in India since the owner thereof was not located in India at the time of the transaction.
- The Delhi High Court thus turned down the view taken by the AAR and held that the income accruing to the petitioner from the transfer of its right, title or interest in and to the trademarks in Foster's brand intellectual property is not taxable in India under the Income-tax Act, 1961.

Conclusion

The Delhi High Court, reversing the AAR ruling, has held that in the absence of any specific provision in the Act for the location of an intangible capital asset such as trademarks, brands, logos, etc., the situs of intangible assets are to be determined by the situs of the owner of the intangible assets. Further it was held that the income received from the transfer of rights, title or interest in the IPRs is not taxable in India as the *situs* of the IPR is not in India.

Formula One World Championship Ltd v. CIT (Int. Tax.) (2017)

Court: Supreme Court, India

This case[69] deals with the issue of fixed place permanent establishment (PE) in a scenario where the duration of the taxable event was very short.

Background/Facts

- FOWC, the taxpayer and a UK resident company; the Federation Internationale de I' automobile (FIA), an international motor sports events regulating association; and Formula One Asset Management Limited (FOAM) entered into certain agreements whereby FOAM licensed all commercial rights in the FIA Formula One World Championship (Championship) to FOWC for a period of 100 years with effect from January 1, 2011.
- The taxpayer entered into a race promotion contract (RPC) with Jaypee Sports International Ltd (Jaypee) on September 13, 2011, under which it granted the right to host, stage and promote the Formula One Grand Prix of India event at the Buddh International Circuit in Noida for a consideration of $40 million. The Concorde Agreement was signed between FIA, FOA and FOWC whereby not only FOWC became Commercial Rights Holder for 100 years.
- An artwork licence agreement (ALA) was also entered into between FOWC and Jaypee on the same day under which FOWC permitted Jaypee to use certain marks and intellectual property belonging to FOWC for a consideration of $1 million.
- Various other agreements were also entered into between the parties to give effect to their understanding relating to the racing event in India.
- Both FOWC and Jaypee approached the Authority for Advance Rulings (AAR) to determine their tax position.
- The AAR concluded that the consideration received by FOWC is in the nature of royalty as FOWC does not have a fixed place of business/PE in India.

69. [2017] 291 CTR 24 (Delhi).

- FOWC filed a writ challenging AAR's ruling on the issue of royalty, and Revenue [Commissioner of Income-tax, (International Taxation)] also filed a writ challenging AAR's ruling on the issue of FOWC not having a PE in India.
- The High Court reversed AAR's findings on both the issues. It held that the amount received by FOWC would not be treated as royalty and that FOWC had a PE in India; therefore, the consideration received shall be taxable in India.

Key arguments of the taxpayer

- The Buddh International Circuit was not at the disposal of the taxpayer (FOWC). Jaypee was responsible for conducting the event and had complete control over it.
- The duration for which FOWC was granted access to the race venue was not sufficient to constitute the degree of permanence necessary to establish a fixed place PE in India.

Issues for consideration before Supreme Court

The Supreme Court was required to examine the entire gamut of agreements between the parties to adjudicate the characterisation. Further, it was also required to adjudicate on withholding tax and attribution issues.

Ruling of the Supreme Court

The Court's observations on the factual matrix of the case are as follows:

- Buddh International Circuit — a fixed place — is the venue of different races, including the F-1 Grand Prix; and the income generated from these events constitutes an economic/business activity. The commercial rights vested with FOWC were exploited to conduct the event in India. FOWC and its affiliates had physical control of the circuit, including the paddock and participating teams, from start to finish of the event.
- Against FOWC's contention that the event duration was only three days, the Apex Court observed:
- The race was to be conducted only for three days in a year; but for the entire period of the race, FOWC had full control and exclusive access to the circuit.

- The duration of the agreement was five years, which was extendable to another five years.
    - o The control over the venue, i.e., Buddh International Circuit, continued at least two weeks before and one week after the event.
    - o The question of the PE has to be examined keeping in mind that the aforesaid race was to be conducted only for three days in a year and for the entire period of race the control was with FOWC.
- The Court noted that a PE has to be a fixed place of business 'through' which the business of an enterprise is wholly or partly carried out. The fixed place of business need not be owned or leased by the foreign enterprise, but it shall be at the disposal of the foreign enterprise in the sense of having some right to use the premises for the purposes of its business.
- Referring to Queen's Counsel Philip Baker's commentary, the Court held that a PE must have three characteristics — stability, productivity, and dependence. The Court extensively relied on the OECD commentary, commentaries of international tax authors, and leading domestic and international judicial precedents for adjudicating the PE issue.

The Court concluded:

- Buddh International Circuit is a fixed place where the commercial/economic activity of conducting the F-1 Championship is carried out; it, therefore, was a virtual projection of the FOWC in India.
- In the present case, all the characteristics mentioned above for a PE — stability, productivity, and dependence — are present. A fixed place of business in the form of physical location, i.e., Buddh International Circuit, was at the disposal of FOWC through which it conducted its business.
- If Jaypee is the event promoter, which owns the title to the circuit in the sense that it owns the land, FOWC is the commercial rights owner of the event, by virtue of the Concorde Agreement.

- FOWC earned in India through the said track over which it had complete control during the period of the race.
    - o The peculiarity of this activity provided in the agreement is such that FOWC's dominant role is evident.
- FOWC earned in India through the said track over which it had complete control during the period of the race.
- The taxable event had taken place in India; therefore, FOWC is liable to pay tax in India on the income earned in India.
- On attribution of income taxable in India, the Court held that the portion of FOWC's income that is attributable to the Indian PE would be treated as its business income to be taxed in India.
- The Supreme Court also held that as far as the issue of default in deducting Indian withholding tax is concerned, it will be to the extent of profits considered attributable/taxable in India.

Conclusion

The Supreme Court's decision is of considerable importance to furthering international tax jurisprudence. The taxpayer will need to take cognisance of the principles laid down by the Court for fixed place PE in India. The Court has ruled that the provisions relating to collection and deposit of tax *via* Tax Deducted at Source for non-resident payments are integral to the scheme of the Income-Tax Act, 1961 and need to be appropriately considered while giving effect to such transactions.

Income-tax Officer, Ward 12 (2), Kolkata v. Right Florists (P.) Ltd (2013)

Court: Income-tax Appellate Tribunal, Kolkata

This case[70] deals with the taxability of payments made to foreign search engine portals for online advertising services.

Background/Facts

- The assessee, Right Florists (P.) Ltd, used online platforms, i.e., Google and Yahoo, for advertising/promotional marketing, but did not deduct tax at source while making payments to the digital service providers.

70. 2013 (25) ITR (Trib) 639 (Kolkata).

- The Assessing Officer disallowed payments under section 40(a)(i) for non-deduction of tax at source, holding the amount as taxable in the hands of the digital service providers/search engine companies.
- On appeal, the Commissioner (Appeals) deleted the disallowance on the ground that Google and Yahoo did not have any permanent establishment in India and, therefore, the amounts were not taxable in view of the provisions of the DTAA with Ireland and USA. Aggrieved, Revenue preferred an appeal.

Observations of Kolkata Tribunal

Nature of transaction

- Google and Yahoo search engines are basically software codes designed to search information on the internet. When online users need information about a product or service, they visit the websites of these search engines and key in the search words for which a large number of results, such as addresses of the related websites are displayed. Users can then visit those websites for more information on the product or service.
- Sponsored search, on the other hand, is de facto advertising that enables advertisers to enhance visibility of their websites. The actual rendering of the service is a technical process, where the web search engine maintains real-time information by running an algorithm on a web crawler to display sponsored advertisement prominently in the search results. The search engine is, primarily, paid to divert traffic to the sponsored website.
- An ad server, at the core of this form of online advertising, is a computer server, specifically a web server that stores advertisements used in online marketing and delivers them to website visitors. Whatever be the form of advertising service, whether sponsored or as a web banner or in any other form, there can hardly be any dispute on the proposition that these search engines or ad servers, which are patented and provide valuable services, are essentially technical in nature. It is this kind of advertising service for which the payments were made by the assessee.

Observations and ruling of the Kolkata Tribunal

- To examine the taxability of an income in the hands of a non-resident, these three aspects need to be examined — application of section 5(2)(a), application of section 5(2)(b), and application of section 9, which actually deal with the deeming fiction embedded in section 5(2)(b). In the present case, it is an admitted position that the payment was not received or deemed to have been received in India. Section 5(2)(a), therefore, has no application in the matter. Therefore, the scope of section 5(2)(b), i.e., "income accruing or arising in India" and "income deemed to accrue or arise in India", needs to be considered.
- The Supreme Court, in the case of *CIT* v. *Hyundai Heavy Industries Co. Ltd* (2007)[71], inter alia observed that, "… as far as the income accruing or arising in India, an income which accrues or arises to a foreign enterprise in India can be only such portion of income accruing or arising to such a foreign enterprise as is attributable to its business carried out in India. This business could be carried out through its branch(es) or through some other form of its presence in India such as office, project site, factory, sales outlet, etc. (hereinafter called as 'PE of foreign enterprise')…"
- A search engine's presence in a location, other than the location of its effective place of management, is only on the internet or by way of a website, which is not a form of physical presence. As to whether a website can be a PE or not, guidance is found from the High-Powered Committee Report[72] which, while recognising the need to make the form of presence tax neutral but realising the limitations of the scope of existing principles and rules, observed, "The Committee supports the view that the concept of PE should be abandoned and a serious attempt should be made within the OECD or the UN to find an alternative to the concept of PE". Clearly, conventional PE tests fail in this virtual world even when a reasonable level of commercial activity is crossed by a foreign enterprise.

71. (2007) 7 SCC 422.
72. The High-Powered Committee (HPC) on 'Electronic Commerce and Taxation' was constituted by the Central Board of Direct Taxes on December 16, 1999.

- In the light of the above discussions, even as per the High-Powered Committee, a website per se, which is the only form of Google's presence in India — as far as test of primary meaning, i.e., basic rule, of PE is concerned — cannot be a permanent establishment under domestic law. This view further finds support from the commentary on the OECD Model Convention.

- The interpretation of the expression 'permanent establishment', even in the context of tax treaties, therefore, does not normally extend to websites unless the servers on which websites are hosted are also located in the same jurisdiction. While a website per se does not constitute a tangible property as it cannot have a location which constitutes a place of business, a web server, on which the website is stored and through which it is accessible, is a piece of equipment having a physical location and such location may, thus, constitute a 'fixed place of business' of the enterprise that operates that server. A search engine, which has only its presence through its website, therefore, cannot be a permanent establishment unless its web servers are also located in the same jurisdiction. That is not the situation here and it is not the case of the Revenue that servers are located in India.

- In view of the above discussions, Google's presence in India through its website cannot be said to constitute a permanent establishment in India under the basic rule and, thus, conditions of section 5(2)(b), read with the Supreme Court's judgement in the *case of Hyundai Heavy Industries Co. Ltd* (2007)[73], are not satisfied to the extent that no profits can be said to accrue or arise in India.

- Thus, the question remains whether the second limb of section 5(2)(b), i.e., income "deemed to accrue or arise in India", can be invoked in this case. So far as this deeming fiction[74] is concerned, a complete code of this deeming fiction has been spelt out in section 9 and Section 9(1), specifying the incomes that shall be deemed to accrue or arise in India. Clause (i) of section 9(1) provides that all income accruing or arising, whether directly or indirectly, through or from any business connection in India, or through or from any

73. (2007) 7 SCC 422.
74. Deeming fiction means law considers a particular thing in a particular way, although in general parlance it is not understood in that sense.

property in India or through or from any asset or source of income in India, etc., shall be deemed to have accrued or arisen in India. In the present case, the Assessing Officer has not made such a claim nor was it pointed out that how the receipts have arisen on account of any business connection in India. There was nothing on record to demonstrate or suggest that the online advertising revenues generated in India were supported by, serviced by or connected with any entity based in India. On these facts, the Tribunal held that section 9(1)(i) cannot have any application in the matter.

- Section 9(1)(ii), (iii), (iv) and (v) deal with incomes in the nature of salaries, dividend and interest, etc., and therefore, these deeming fictions are not applicable to the facts of the case. As far as applicability of section 9(1)(vi) is concerned, co-ordinate benches, in the cases of *Pinstorm Technologies (P.) Ltd* v. *ITO* (2012)[75] and *Yahoo India (P.) Ltd*[76], have concluded that the provisions of section 9(1)(vi) cannot be invoked. That leaves out only section 9(1)(vii).
- In view of the provision of section 9(1)(vii), if services rendered by the foreign enterprise by way of online advertising services constitute technical services, the income from providing these services can be taxed under section 9(1)(vii). It is also not necessary that services should be rendered in India. It is also relevant that the definition of 'fees for technical services' under the India-Ireland DTAA agreement (India-Irish tax treaty, in short) is on the same lines as in the Income-tax Act and does not have a 'make available' clause. The 'fees for technical service', which is also taxable in the source jurisdiction under the India-Irish tax treaty at a rate not exceeding 10%, is defined under Article 12(2)(b) as "payment of any kind in consideration for the rendering of any managerial, technical or consultancy services including the provision of services by technical or other personnel …". The scope of fees for technical services (FTS) in the tax treaty is, thus, not any narrower than the scope under domestic tax law. It is, therefore, essential to examine whether or not the online advertising services in question can be said to be technical services of a nature that can be covered by the scope of explanation 2 to section 9(1)(vii).

---

75. TS 536 ITAT (2012) Mum.
76. *Yahoo India P. Ltd.* v. *DCIT*, (2011) 140 TTJ (Mum) 195.

- While there is no specific definition assigned to technical services, explanation 2 to section 9(1)(vii), as also Article 12 (2)(b), merely states that 'fees for technical services' will include considering of "rendering of any managerial, technical or consultancy services". It is significant that the expression 'technical' appears along with the expressions 'managerial' and 'consultancy', and all the three words refer to various types of services, consideration for which is included in the scope of 'fees for technical services'. The significance of this company of words has been discussed by the co-ordinate bench of this tribunal in the case of *Kotak Securities Ltd* v. *Dy. CIT* (2012)[77] and by the Delhi High Court in the case of *CIT* v. *Bharti Cellular Ltd* (2009, 2008)[78]. As per this decision, both the words managerial and consultancy involve a human element. And both, managerial services and consultancy services are provided by humans. Consequently, applying the rule of '*noscitur a sociis*',[79] the word 'technical' as appearing in explanation 2 to section 9(1)(vii) would also have to be construed as involving a human element.

- The service rendered by Google is the generation of certain text on the search engine result page. This is a wholly automated process. In the light of the legal position that any services rendered without a human touch, even if it be a technical service, cannot be a technical service covered by the limited scope of section 9(1)(vii), the receipts for online advertisement by the search engines cannot be treated as fees for technical services taxable as income, under the provisions of the Income-tax Act, in the hands of Google. The wordings of explanation 2 to section 9(1)(vii) as also that of the definition of fees for technical services under Article 12(2)(b) being similar in material respects, the above legal proposition equally applies to the definition under Article 12(2)(b) of the India-Irish tax treaty. The income earned by Google, in respect of online advertising revenues discussed above, and based on the facts on record, cannot be brought to tax as income deemed to accrue or arise under section 9(1)(vii), i.e., the last limb of section 9(1), as well.

---

77. [2012] 50 SOT 158 (Mum).
78. [2008] 319 ITR 139 (Del).
79. The rule of *noscitur a sociis* implies that the meaning of an unclear word may be known from its accompanying words.

- The facts relating to Yahoo being similar in material aspects, the same conclusion holds good for Yahoo as well. In addition, as Yahoo is a USA-based Delaware company, the benefit of 'make available' clause under Indo-USA tax treaty may also apply.

- The connotations of the expression 'make available' were examined by the Tribunal in the case of *Raymond Ltd* v. *Dy. CIT* (2003)[80]. There are two high Court decisions — that of the Delhi High Court in the case of *DIT* v. *Guy Carpenter & Co Ltd* (2012)[81] and of the Karnataka High Court in the case of *CIT* v. *De Beers India Minerals (P.) Ltd* (2012)[82]. These uphold the principle that unless services rendered by the service provider result in transfer of technology and enable the recipient of service to make use of the technical knowledge by himself and without recourse to the service provider, mere rendition of such services cannot be brought to tax as fees for technical service.

- Clearly, as far as online advertising is concerned, there is no transfer of any technology of any kind, and as such any payment for such service is outside the ambit of source taxation under Article 12. For this reason, the payments made to Yahoo could not be brought to tax in India.

- Therefore, the receipts in respect of online advertising on Google and Yahoo cannot be brought to tax in India under the provisions of the Income-tax Act, 1961, as also under the provisions of the India-US and the India-Ireland tax treaties. This observation is subject to the rider that as far as the PE issue is concerned, the existence of PE has been examined only on the basis of website *simplicitor* and on no other additional basis, as no case was made out for the same. In any case, Revenue has not brought anything on record, either at the assessment stage or even before the Tribunal, to suggest that Google or Yahoo had a PE in India.

- In view of the above discussions and considering the entirety of the case, the Tribunal held that there was no failure in deduction of tax at source by the assessee as long as the assessee did not have any

80. [2003] 86 ITD 791 (Mum).
81. (2012) 346 ITR 504.
82. 346 ITR 467 (Kar).

obligation to deduct tax at source under section 195 for the simple reason that income embedded in impugned payments was not chargeable to tax in India. Accordingly, the disallowance under section 40(a)(i) was uncalled for.

Conclusion

The Kolkata Tribunal applied the basic rule to ascertain if a non-resident had a PE in India, which is based on the physical presence of the website/ equipment and ruled that in the absence of a server/website in India, there cannot be a PE. As regards the issue of royalty, the Tribunal followed the co-ordinate bench ruling in the case of Pinstorm and Yahoo and held that Google's and Yahoo's online advertising services do not give rise to royalties. Finally, the Tribunal also held that such services are not fees for technical services due to the lack of human intervention in both Google's and Yahoo's cases, and the services do not satisfy the 'make available' clause in the case of Yahoo.

Western Union Financial Services Inc. v. ACIT (2007)

Court: Income Tax Appellate Tribunal, Delhi

This case[83] examines the question of business connection and permanent establishment with respect to money transfer business. It specifically deals with dependent agent's permanent establishment (PE).

Background/Facts

- The assessee, a non-residential company incorporated in the USA, was engaged in the business of rendering money transfer services worldwide. Under the arrangement, any resident of USA desirous of transferring monies to his/her relatives in India would approach the assessee's outlets in the USA with the money, together with charges, for which a receipt with a computer-generated unique number (MTCN) would be given to the remitter for onward transmission to his/her relative in India, who would take it to the assessee's representative/agent in India.

83. (2006) 101 TTJ (Delhi) 56.

- The said agent, in turn, would feed the allotted MTCN into the computer with the help of the software, Voyager, gaining access to the assessee's mainframe computer in the USA. Thereafter, he/she would make the payment to the claimant after ascertaining his/her bona fides through documentary evidence. On completion of the transaction, the agent was to be remunerated by the assessee by way of a commission at an agreed percentage for his/her services.
- For the purpose of carrying out business in India, the assessee entered into agreements appointing four types of agents in India — the Department of Posts, commercial banks, non-banking financial companies, and tour operators. Generally, the appointments were for an initial period of five years, which could be extended any number of times for periods of one year at a time.
- According to the agreement, the money so transferred by the assessee was required to be first paid out by those agents, after which they would be reimbursed the amount together with the commission due to them, which was called the base commission in the agreement. The agents were given the power to appoint sub-agents at their own cost but their services could be terminated by the assessee if it was found that the appointed sub-agent was acting in a manner prejudicial to its interest.
- Pursuant thereto, after obtaining requisite permission from the Reserve Bank of India (RBI), the assessee set up its liaison office (LO) with its own stipulation that it would not represent any party other than the assessee. Thereafter, in accordance with legal requirements and the arrangements with the agents, the assessee kept the RBI posted on the activities of its LO and started remitting monies to India followed by commission payable thereon as remuneration. However, the assessee did not file its return on the ground that it was not taxable in India; but ultimately filed the return, declaring nil income pursuant to the notice issued under section 142(1).
- The Assessing Officer, holding that the income arising to the assessee in India from activities carried out in India was taxable both under the Act and the agreement (DTAA) between India and the USA, framed its assessment accordingly. On appeal, the Commissioner (Appeals) upheld the impugned order. Being aggrieved, the assessee filed an appeal before the Tribunal.

Arguments of the Revenue

- The transaction of remitting monies to India from abroad is a single unified transaction and cannot be severed into two or more transactions, so as to say that at the Indian border it assumes a different character. Both the receiving aspect and the payment aspect are a single integrated whole, incapable of being split.
- The assessee had a business connection in India, as it had a full-fledged office, which conducted aggressive marketing activities together with negotiations with agents, providing software to them and imparting training about the product. The money is paid to the recipient in India on behalf of Western Union by its agents in India and thus, there was no difference between various branches of banks engaging in international transactions and the system adopted by the assessee. There is continuity of the transaction, which gets completed only when the money is paid to the claimant in India through the agents. The software through which the agents access the mainframe computer in the USA is owned by the assessee. Besides, the assessee's employees supervise the transactions. Thus, there is 'business connection' in India, and the assessee is liable under section 9(1) of the Income-tax Act, 1961 to pay income tax on the profits arising from its activities in India.
- The assessee has a PE in India in the form of software installed at agents' premises to conduct business. The software ensures connectivity between the assessee and the premises of the agents who are 'dependent agents' within the meaning of Article 5.4(a) of the DTAA. For instance, the agreement between the assessee and a third party, Weizmann Ltd, prohibits the latter from carrying on a similar business during the term of the agreement and for six months after the agreement's expiry, which shows that Weizmann is working wholly and exclusively for the assessee. The same is the case with other agents. Thus, they are all dependent agents of the assessee and have the authority to conclude contracts on the assessee's behalf in the sense that they carry out in India the commitment given by the assessee to pay the money to the rightful claimant.

- The LO of the assessee in India is involved in marketing, brand building, providing software to agents, and appointing and training them. Therefore, the LO is a PE of the assessee in India.
- It further submitted that so far as the Department of Posts is concerned, appointed as an agent of the assessee in India, though it was engaged in the money order business facilitating transfer of funds within India, the activity of paying out monies in India in the course of 'trans-border money transfer business' was not in the ordinary course of its business, and hence, the primary condition of the article was not fulfilled. It was further pointed out that clause 3.1 of the agreement with the Department of Posts shows that it is a new business in which it had not so far engaged.

  In the case of banks that were appointed as agents, the Tax Department pointed out that though under section 6(1)(a) of the Banking Regulation Act, 1949, banks are allowed to carry on the business of 'collecting and transmitting money', since the said Act extends only to India under section 1(2) thereof, the money transfer business involving trans-border transfer of funds cannot be said to be in the ordinary course of banking business. Hence, banks have had to seek the approval of the RBI under section 3(c) of the Foreign Exchange Management Act, 1999. A similar argument was advanced for non-banking financial companies (NBFCs) and tour operators appointed as the assessee's agents.
- The compensation paid out to the agents for the work was not commensurate to the revenue received by the assessee. As the crux of the transaction — payment of money to the claimant — is carried out by agents in India, it merits adequate compensation. Since the compensation is inadequate, the transaction is not at arm's length.
- The assessee had not submitted its global accounts or balance sheet or India-specific accounts. The only information provided was the amount of transfer and commission paid. Considering the expenses incurred such as network maintenance, communication charges, mainframe expenses, etc., the profit attributable to the Indian operations had been estimated at 10% of the gross commission.

Arguments of the Assessee

- The LO cannot be regarded as a PE since the RBI prohibits carrying on any business or commercial or trading activity under the conditions imposed for granting approval. The activities of the LO are continuously monitored by the RBI, which has not alleged any violations of the relevant conditions. It was pointed out that the LO is manned by only two employees at a junior level with a small staff.
- The assessee relied on the case of *IAC* v. *Mitsui & Co. Ltd*[84] (1991), wherein a Special Bench at Delhi has held that an LO cannot be regarded as a PE. A similar view was taken by the Delhi Bench in *BKI/HAM V.O.F.* v. *ACIT*[85](2001).
- The software alleged to be a PE cannot be so regarded as the agents used the software only to gain access to the assessee's mainframe, located outside India, so that they could match the MTCN number, without which the claimant would not be paid the money. Thus, the software was only a tool to verify the genuineness of the claim and nothing more. The intellectual property rights in the software remained with the assessee. The mere use thereof, it was argued, cannot lead to the result that the premises where it is being used can be regarded as the PE of the assessee. The assessee has no access as of right to the offices or premises of its agents or representatives in India.
- The terms of the agreement did not authorise agents to conclude contracts on the assessee's behalf and not a single instance existed where an agent or representative had concluded any contract for the assessee. The assessee authorised the agents to appoint sub-agents but only to enable the agents to carry on their part of the transaction. Moreover, the assessee had no say or control in the appointment, remuneration, or termination of sub-agents; an activity independently and exclusively managed by the agents.
- The assessee argued that the agents were acting in the ordinary course of their business in undertaking the activity of disbursing payments in India; this activity constituted a fraction of the agents' overall

84. *Inspecting Assistant Commissioner v. Mitsui and Co. Ltd.*, [1991] 39 ITD 59 (Delhi).
85. *BKI/HAM V.O.F. c/o Arthur Anderson & Co. v. Additional Commissioner of Income Tax*, (2001) 70 TTJ (Del) 480.

activities, as they were not devoted wholly or almost wholly for the foreign enterprise (the assessee). The compensation paid to agents is uniform throughout the world, and thus, the dealings between the assessee and the agents were at arm's length. Hence, it cannot be said that the agents were not independent agents.

- The non-compete clause in the agreement of appointment of agent does not make the agent dependent on the foreign enterprise (assessee). It is the usual clause found in all such arrangements, mainly intended to protect the assessee. The training of the agents is an activity auxiliary or preparatory and, therefore, by virtue of Article 5.3(e) of the DTAA, the LO cannot be deemed to be a PE.
- The words "ordinary course of their business" appearing in Article 5.5 of the treaty should be construed broadly, and it must be accordingly held that the agents' activity constituted their regular business. There is no allegation that any of the conditions prescribed by any law were violated, nor is there any evidence to show that the transactions were not at arm's length. Therefore, the agents were all independent agents. It is only because the RBI has been constituted as the ultimate controlling authority for transactions involving foreign remittances that its permission is required under section 3(c) of the FEMA. It does not necessarily mean that the activity is not in the ordinary course of the business of the assessee or representative.
- As regards attribution of profits under Article 7.1 of the DTAA, reference was made to the Supreme Court judgement in the case of *Carborandum Co.*[86] (1977), rendered with reference to section 42(3) of the 1922, Act, the provisions of which now find place in explanation (a) to section 9(1) of the Income Tax Act, 1961. It was contended that it was only those profits that can be reasonably attributed to the Indian operations of the foreign enterprise that can be taxed; and if it can be shown, as explained in Board's circular dated July 23, 1969, that the agent's commission fully represents the value of the profit attributable to his/her service, it should prima facie extinguish the assessment. It was submitted that the compensation paid to the agents at the rate of 25%–30% of the fee, received by the

86. *Carborandum Co. and Ors. v. Commissioner of Income Tax, Madras*, [1977] 108 ITR 335 (SC).

assessee, is a reasonable attribution of the income to the PE (agents), and if the compensation so paid is allowed as a deduction, it will extinguish the assessment.

Decision of the Tribunal

- The case has to be approached first from the point of view of the Act to see if any tax liability arises. In case no tax liability arises under the Act, nothing further requires to be done. But if there is a tax liability arising under the Act, it is open to the non-resident to claim that there is either no or less tax liability if the provisions of the DTAA are applied, in which case the DTAA provisions have to be given effect in preference to the provisions of the Act.
- In *CIT* v. *R.D. Aggarwal & Co.*[87](1965), the Supreme Court held that the expression 'business connection' means something more than a business; that it presupposes an element of continuity between the business of the non-resident and the activity in the taxable territory, although a stray or isolated transaction would not be taken into account; that the connection may take several forms; that it may include carrying on a part of the main business or activity incidental to the non-resident's business through an agent or it may merely be a relation between the business of the non-resident and the activity in the taxable territory that facilitates or assists carrying on of that business.
- Applying these tests in the present case and taking into account the fact that the term 'business connection' is broad in scope, the assessee would have a business connection. The business of the assessee is to transfer monies across countries. Thus, a receiving aspect and a paying aspect exist to the transaction, which cannot be segregated. The transaction, as has been rightly noted by the income-tax authorities, is not complete unless the monies are paid in India to the claimant. Further, the agreements with the agents are initially for a term of five years, renewable for periods of one year at a time, but this could go on indefinitely. The agents are bound to render services for the assessee as stipulated in the agreement, which provides for

87. *Commissioner of Income Tax, Punjab v. R.D. Aggarwal and Company*, [1965] 56 ITR 20 (SC).

security and confidentiality. The assessee has provided the software to the agents, although it retained the copyright, to enable them to access the assessee's mainframes in the USA. All these sufficiently justify the conclusion that there is a business connection within the meaning of section 9(1) of the Act.

Fixed place PE

A PE should project the foreign enterprise in India. The assessee has appointed different agents in India that are the Department of Posts of the Government of India, commercial banks, non-banking financial companies, and tour operators. These agents have their own or hired premises from which they operate. All that they have to do for claiming to be agents of the assessee is to put up a display board. This cannot by any stretch of imagination amount to projection of the assessee in India. It cannot be postulated that post offices of the Department of Posts would permit themselves to be looked upon as projecting the presence of Western Union Financial Services Inc., in India. The same rationale is applicable to commercial banks and others that have been appointed as agents. They have their own presence and business with which they are, perhaps, more concerned and may be surprised to find themselves characterised as projecting the assessee on Indian soil. There is no evidence to show that the assessee can, as a matter of right, enter and make use of the premises of these agents for its business. Therefore, there is no fixed place PE of the assessee in India.

Is LO a fixed place PE?

The LO acted as a communication link between the agents and the assessee's head office. After obtaining RBI's approval, it appointed agents, and offered training and refresher courses relating to the assessee's operations, such as expected standards of service and security, accounting procedures, telecommunication systems and configuration, merchandising standards, as well as publishing publicity material like posters for display at the agents' locations. Further, the LO facilitated the visit of the Director (Operations) of the assessee to the agents' premises so that they could satisfy themselves about quality standards. The LO also provided training on using the management software (Voyager) to agents (free of cost) and their staff. These activities are in line with the activities mentioned in the annexure to the application made to the RBI, seeking permission to open the LO. The annexure also stated the activities that would not be undertaken by the LO, and there are no allegations of any violation of the conditions of approval.

The LO cannot be considered to be the fixed place PE of the assessee as it carries out activities which are of a preparatory or auxiliary character. It has not carried on any trading activity for the assessee in India. It has only a small number of executives and a support staff. The LO has also filed status reports to the RBI, listing out the activities which it actually carried on during the years.

In *Re: UAE Exchange Centre LLC* v. *Unknown*[88] (2004), the AAR noticed that the applicant, who was engaged in money transfer business, had adopted the mode of remitting money to India through its liaison offices in India. The liaison offices downloaded the data about beneficiaries in India, printed cheques/drafts and dispatched them to the beneficiaries. On these facts, it was held that the LOs constituted PE in India.

The test laid down by the AAR was that the LO's role should be nothing short of performing the contract of remitting amounts at least in part before it could be called a PE of the foreign enterprise. Remitting amounts, at least in part, was held to constitute an essential activity in performing the contractual obligation and it did not constitute an auxiliary activity. In the present case, the LO performs no part of the contract of remitting the money into India. The nature of the LO's activities can at best be called auxiliary or preparatory in nature. Therefore, the LO cannot be considered to be the PE of the assessee in India.

Software as the PE of the assessee

The agents operate from owned or hired premises, and there was no evidence to show that the assessee could, as a matter of right, enter and use the premises for its business. The software is the assessee's property, and it has not parted with its copyright therein in favour of the agents. The agents have only been allowed to use it in order to gain access to the mainframe computers in the USA.

Mere use of the software at agents' premises cannot lead to the premises-cum-software to be the assessee's PE in India. Under Article 5, installation may amount to a PE if used for exploring natural resources. Even if the

88. (2004) 268 ITR 9 AAR.

software is considered as an installation, it cannot per se be treated as a PE because it is not used for exploring or exploiting natural resources.

Agency PE

Three conditions must be met for an agent to qualify as an independent agent: (1) He/She should be acting in the ordinary course of his/her business, (2) his/her activities should not be devoted wholly or almost wholly on behalf of the foreign enterprise for whom he/she is acting as agent, and (3) the transactions between the foreign enterprise and the agent should be at arm's length.

(1) He/she should be acting in the ordinary course of his/her business

In the leading case of *Narain Swadeshi Weaving Mills* v. *CEPT*[89] (1954), the Supreme Court explained that business connotes some real, substantive and systematic course of activity or conduct with a set purpose. In *Liquidators of Pursa Ltd* v. *CIT*[90] (1954), the Supreme Court held that underlying the expression 'business' is the fundamental idea of continuous exercise of an activity. In *Barendra Prasad Ray* v. *ITO*[91] (1981), the Supreme Court again held that the word is of wide import and means an activity carried on continuously and systematically by a person by applying his/her labour and skill with a view to earning income. Therefore, any activity which is systematically and continuously carried on with the object of earning profits is a business activity.

In this way, the agents' activity of paying monies to beneficiaries or claimants in India, after verifying their identities as well as accessing the MTCN number to validate the genuineness of the claim, amounts to conducting the business of money transfer. The agreement of an agent is initially for a period of five years and can be renewed for successive periods of one year each. The agents could appoint sub-agents for carrying out the activity. They have to maintain records and measure up

89. *Narain Swadeshi Weaving Mills* v. *The Commissioner of Excess Profits Tax,* [1954] 26 ITR 765 (SC).
90. *The Liquidators of Pursa Limited* v. *Commissioner of Income Tax, Bihar,* [1954] 25 ITR 265 (SC).
91. *Barendra Prasad Ray and Ors.* v. *Income Tax Officer and Ors.*, [1981] 129 ITR 295.

to the standards set by the assessee. They have received training from the assessee in the use of the software and communication systems. All these are activities are carried on systematically and continuously with a set purpose and hence amount to business.

In the case of the Department of Posts, it is well known that they accept money orders for transfer of funds within India. Engaging in a similar business with international ramifications is just an extension of their business. It cannot be said that it is not in the ordinary course of their business. The same rationale applies to commercial banks. Although, strictly speaking, it may not be part of their banking business as defined in the Banking Regulation Act, 1949, they have obtained RBI's approval under section 3(c) of the Foreign Exchange Management Act (FEMA) to carry it out. Although the approval is only for the purpose of FEMA, it would still amount to a business, though not banking business, because it has been carried on systematically and continuously to earn a commission. Given the multiple services provided by banks these days, all with a business motive, it is difficult to say that the activity carried on by the assessee's agents in India is not a business activity in the ordinary course of their business. Non-banking financial companies deal with money belonging to others and the activity of paying out monies on behalf of the Western Union Financial Services Inc., must be viewed as part of their business activity. In the case of tour operators, acting as agents of an established firm engaged in international money transfers may be conducive to their business. A broad view needs to be taken in these matters.

(2) Activities should not be devoted wholly or almost wholly on behalf of the foreign enterprise for which he/she is acting as agent

The Department of Posts functions under the aegis of the concerned Ministry of the Government of India. Its main activity is to serve the public in India for sending/receiving letters, parcels, packets, etc., within or to/from outside India, money orders within India, maintaining small savings account in several forms such as savings certificates, time-deposit accounts, postal life insurance, etc. The Department, with a vast network across the country, is a service organisation for the general public's benefit, and it would be a misnomer to say that its activities are wholly or almost wholly devoted to the US-based Western Union Financial Services Inc. There is no evidence that the Department of Posts is dependent on the assessee for its revenues, and the same is the case with commercial banks, non-banking financial companies, and tour operators appointed as the assessee's agents.

Moreover, there is no evidence to show that the extent of their activities for the assessee, compared to all their activities, is so large that it can be said that they are dependent on the assessee for their earnings or revenues. The agents in the present case have not been shown to be economically dependent on the assessee. They are not carrying on the activity for the assessee, as agents, in exclusion of their other businesses or activities. In this situation, it cannot be said that their activities are wholly or almost wholly devoted to the assessee just because they are not acting as agents for any other company in the money transfer business. Further, an agent will in no case be liable for damages for the delay, non-payment or underpayment of the money transfer. The agent is not, therefore, liable to any risk on this account.

(3) The transactions between the foreign enterprise and the agent should be at arm's length

As per the agreement, 'base compensation' is 30% in the case of the Department of Posts and 25% for others. The compensation may be reduced for the Department of Posts if the assessee were to assume responsibility for advertising and promotion of services or to establish a customer service centre. The reduction, however, shall not exceed 10% of the gross revenues earned by the agent concerned from the money transfer business done by it in the relevant year. In the case of banks appointed as agents, the assessee can determine the amount of reduction. There is no material evidence to show that the rates of compensation are higher in other cases so as to indicate that the agents were discriminated against. The higher rate of compensation in the case of the Department of Posts is probably because its reach is much wider compared to commercial banks, NBFCs or tour operators. The terms of appointment of sub-agents are uniform in all cases. Thus, there seems to be no basis for the charge that the compensation paid is not adequate for the services rendered by the agents. There is no finding contrary to the claim made by the assessee that the rates of compensation are uniform throughout the world. In these circumstances, there is no merit in the claim that the transactions between the assessee and the agents are not at arm's length.

No express authority is given to the agents in the agreement. All that the income-tax authorities have stated is that (a) the agents carry out in India the commitment given by the assessee to the remitter of the money abroad, and (b) the agents have the power to appoint sub-agents to do their work. From these facts, taken singly or together, it cannot be inferred that the agents either have the authority to conclude the contracts or have habitually exercised the authority without any protest from the assessee. The fact that the agents (in the present case) have the authority to appoint sub-agents does not mean that they (agents) have the authority to conclude contracts. Nowhere in the sub-agency agreement do agents have any authority to conclude contracts. In fact, when the agents themselves have no such authority under their agreement, they cannot delegate the same to their sub-agents.

The fact that the agents conclude in India the commitment of the assessee made abroad cannot be considered as an authority to conclude contracts. The contract is between the remitter abroad and the assessee. It is entered into outside India. The agents are not party thereto. The agents merely carry out the concluding step in the arrangement embodied in the contract. In other words, the assessee undertakes the responsibility outside India to transfer the money to India. It is only the payment part of the undertaking that is executed by the agents in India. The contract is already concluded outside India. The agent has no say over the contract. He/she has to merely execute the payment part, after ensuring the genuineness of the transaction and verifying the beneficiary's identity in India. By executing the last leg of the contract that has already been concluded (outside India), he/she is not concluding the contract for the assessee. The appointment of sub-agents is merely to facilitate the agent's work. Besides, what is considered to be a 'duty' cannot be considered to be an 'authority'. By making a payment to the beneficiary, the agent in India is only performing his/her duty under the agreement of agency, for which he/she is remunerated; he/she is not exercising any 'authority', certainly not the authority to conclude contracts on behalf of the assessee. The words 'duty' and 'authority' are incompatible. The dictionary meaning of the word 'duty' is "assignment/burden/commitment that one is obliged to do by law or by calling of one's business". It connotes an obligation, which a person is bound to perform. Per contra, 'authority' in law belongs to the province of power. Judged by these tests, the fact that the agents in India pay out the money to the beneficiaries or claimants, which they are bound to under the agreement with the assessee for which they are remunerated, does not appear to be a case of exercise of any authority. Thus, the agents do not habitually exercise the authority to conclude the contracts on behalf of the assessee.

Thus, there is no agency PE of the assessee in India under Article 5 of the DTAA between India and the USA. Thus, no profits can be attributed to the Indian operations of the assessee and taxed in India.

Conclusion

The Tribunal analysed the facts both from the perspective of business connection and permanent establishment. As regards 'business connection', the tests laid down by judicial precedence were noted and it was observed that the expression 'business connection' was wide enough in scope to include the present situation and hence, it was held that the money transfer activity carried out in India by the agents constituted 'business connection'.

It then analysed the question of existence of PE. With respect to fixed place PE, it was observed that the premises of the agents were not at the disposal of the assessee and the agents were carrying on their business. Further, it was observed that the LO was permitted to carry on limited activities for which it was set up in India with RBI's approval, and it does not undertake the money transfer business. It was also observed that the software that gives agents access to the US mainframe computer was owned and belonged to the assessee, and agents only had the right to use it for the limited purpose of agency work. Therefore, there is no fixed place PE of the assessee in India. Further, it was observed that the agents were independent agents as they were not economically dependent on the assessee. They neither had the authority to conclude contracts, as per the agreement, nor did they habitually exercise authority to conclude contracts. Therefore, there is no PE of the assessee in India. As the provisions of the DTAA are more beneficial, the assessee would not be liable for tax in India.

Dell Spain (2012)

Court: Central Economic Administrative Court, Spain

This case[92] deals with a situation wherein a subsidiary, dealing directly with customers on its account under the direct sale model, was brought under the commissionaire model. Under the commissionaire arrangement, the subsidiary, however, was performing the same work as was undertaken earlier. The Spanish Court examined whether such an arrangement would lead to PE of the parent company.

Background/Facts

The US multinational computer technology company Dell's products were manufactured in Ireland by the Irish company, Dell Europe, and sold by the Irish company, Dell Products, through local Dell subsidiaries in various European countries. Dell Products operated through a direct sales model whereby the purchase orders were placed on a web or call centre.

Dell Spain was responsible for the direct sale of computer products in Spain. In charge of the commercialisation of these products, it operated as a full-fledged distributor; Dell Products had no employees or facilities in Spain.

In 1995, the sales operations of the Dell group were reorganised and the customer profile database was transferred to Dell Products, which was responsible for the sale of computers and for managing and controlling distribution in different markets through local distributor companies. These distributors were functionally characterised and remunerated as commissionaires; however, from a business perspective, they actually performed substantive activities beyond a mere commissionaire function. Dell Products did not have its own human resources; they were subcontracted from Dell Europe.

In the new sales structure, Dell's computers were sold in Spain by Dell Spain in the capacity of a commissionaire (unlike the earlier scenario of the direct sale between Dell Spain and customers) under a commission agreement with Dell Products in Ireland as the principal. Dell Spain sold and marketed the computers in the Spanish market in its own name but for the account of

92. Case 00/2107/2007.

Dell Products. In particular, Dell Spain was directly and actively involved in the logistics, marketing, after-sales services and administration of Dell Products' Spanish online store. The Spanish market was segmented into: (a) large customers who required specialised and on-site attention were served by Dell Spain and (b) small-sized customers were served by Dell France through a call centre and a website.

Issues raised before the Court

Whether the way the sales operations in Spain were organised under the commissionaire agreement made Dell Spain a permanent establishment of Dell Products under Article 5(1) [fixed place of business] and/or Article 5(5) [dependent agent] of the tax treaty between Ireland and Spain (the treaty). If so, what is the proportion of its profits that could be attributed to the activities of such PE?

Court's Decision

The issue of fixed place of business

The Spanish Court held that Dell Products had a fixed place of business in Spain through the use of Dell Spain's facilities. The Court observed that according to Para 4 of the OECD commentary on Article 5, it is immaterial whether these facilities are owned or rented by or are otherwise at the disposal of Dell Products. A parent company can have a PE in the state where its subsidiary has a place of business, e.g., a space or premise belonging to the subsidiary that is at the disposal of the parent company.

The Court then dealt with the question of whether the online store could be characterised as an 'online PE', even though the server was situated outside Spain and no activity was performed through human resources or assets located in Spain. The Court observed that the sales and deliveries in Spain by Dell Products through the server in France were economically significant and that employees of Dell Spain were involved in the maintenance of the online store. The Court did not follow the explanation of Paras 42.1 to 42.10 of the OECD commentary on Article 5, where it is stated that a website does not constitute a PE in a state, unless the server is physically located in that state. As the trading, selling and delivery carried out in Spain were economically significant activities, the Court was not prepared to accept these paragraphs of the OECD commentary as guidance in the pertinent case. The Court found support in Para 45.6 of the OECD commentary on Article 5 in which Spain had included an observation on these paragraphs of the OECD commentary, indicating that Spain would not necessarily take into consideration the aforementioned paragraphs until the OECD study of e-commerce taxation has been brought to a final conclusion. (This Spanish observation was withdrawn in the 2010 version of the OECD Model Convention.)

The issue of the agency PE

Furthermore, the Court held that Dell Products had an agency PE in Spain because Dell Spain had the authority to conclude contracts in its name, and hence was acting as a dependent agent. These contracts were binding on Dell Products, even if those contracts were not actually concluded in its name. In this context, the Court took into consideration that Dell Spain acted under the comprehensive supervision and control of Dell Products and its activities were not limited to those of an auxiliary character.

Conclusion

The Central Economic-Administrative Court (TEAC) held in favour of the tax authorities. The Court decided that Dell Spain constituted a Spanish PE of Dell Products, both under Article 5(1) and Article 5(4) of the treaty. The TEAC used the commentaries to the OECD Model as an interpretative guideline. This conclusion was reached despite the fact that Dell Products had no employees or facilities in Spain. The Court held that all the sales by Dell Products in Spain (less commission paid to Dell Spain and other related allocable expenses) should be attributed to Dell Product's Spanish PE. The Court also held that the sales to Spanish customers through the French subsidiary of the Dell group should be allocated to the Spanish PE of Dell Products inasmuch as the sales of the French subsidiary were carried out through or with substantial involvement of the human and material resources of Dell Spain. The Court observed that from a legal and economic perspective, the division of the functions between Dell France and Dell Spain was unclear. In the Court's opinion, tax authorities had sufficiently demonstrated that the most significant economic activities were carried out in Spain.

Taxation of Software - Indian Supreme Court ruling

Recently the Indian Supreme Court held in *Engineering Analysis Centre Pvt Limited* v. *CIT*[93] and host of multiple cases concluded that Income received by Non-Resident on license of software is not taxable in India as the license of software is not Royalty under the definition of domestic tax laws of India i.e., Income-tax Act, 1961 and also under the definition of Royalty under the DTAA.

Issue under litigation

- Taxation of income from computer software programs in international transactions, has been a litigious issue before Indian tax authorities.
- Tax authorities have adopted a position that income arising from transactions involving grant of software program/license should be characterized as "royalty", regardless of the rights in software that are granted.
- The taxpayer's position, on the other hand, has been that characterization as royalty or business profits (especially under an applicable DTAA) should be based on the nature and extent of rights granted to the end user.
- The recent ruling of the Supreme Court adjudicates on 86 appeals filed by multiple assessee's in the context of taxability of payments made by resident Indian end users/ distributors to non-resident computer software manufacturers/ suppliers, for the distribution/use of computer software.

Background of the Supreme Court ruling

To analyse multiple appeals, the Supreme Court categorized facts of all appeals into four categories:

- Category 1- Resident Indian buyers of computer software who purchase this directly from a foreign non-resident supplier
- Category 2- Resident Indian distributors who purchase computer software from non-resident suppliers or manufacturers for the purpose of resale

93. *Engineering Analysis Centre of Excellence Private Limited* v. *The Commissioner of Income Tax and Ors.*, MANU/SC/0137/2021.

- o Category 3 - Non-resident vendors, who, after purchasing software from non-resident sellers, resell the same to resident Indian distributors or end users
- o Category 4 - Non-resident suppliers who affix computer software onto hardware and then sell the same as an integrated unit/equipment to resident Indian distributors/ end users.
    - The question that was before the Supreme Court was whether income derived by foreign non-residents suppliers (supplying software in India), under each of the above categories is in the nature of royalty or not. Where this question would be answered in the affirmative, there would be a charge of income in the hands of non-resident chargeable to tax in India.

Analysis

- To determine taxability of income in the hands non-resident, the Supreme Court, *inter-alia*, evaluated the following parameters:
    - o Reliance on DTAA at the stage of Tax deducted at Source under the provisions section 195 of the Income-Tax Act 1961 (IT Act).[94]
        - ✓ The SC opined that once it is established that a stream of income is taxable in the hands of a non-resident recipient, the provisions of withholding tax will apply. Where there is no charge of income in the hands of non-resident recipient, there is no obligation on the resident payer to withhold taxes.
        - ✓ The principle above was earlier upheld in the case of GE India Technology Centre (P) Ltd[95] and has been re-affirmed in this ruling
        - ✓ While concluding the above the Honourable Supreme Court distinguished the ruling in PILCOM case on this.

94. Under the provisions of section 195 of the Income-Tax Act 1961 every resident of India when it makes payment to non-resident is required to deduct tax at source in respect of income component on the payment due or payable to Non-Resident.
95. (2010) 10 SCC 29.

- ✓ Accordingly, once it is established that non-resident supplier does not have any income chargeable to tax in India, there is no obligation on the part of resident payer to withhold taxes,

- o **Analysis of the term copyright**
  - ✓ A key consideration in these appeals was the extent of right granted by non-resident vendors to resident deductors. Accordingly, the scope of term 'copyright' under the Copyright Act, 1957 (CA) was discussed in detail in the ruling.
  - ✓ Copyright is in an exclusive right, which is negative in nature, being a right to restrict others from doing certain acts.
  - ✓ Owner of a copy right in a software is entitled to grant any interest in his rights by way of a license in lieu of royalty income.
  - ✓ Illustratively, purchaser of a book or a CD/DVD becomes the owner of the physical article but does not become the owner of the copyright inherent in the work. Such copyright remains exclusively with the owner.
  - ✓ Accordingly, where resident distributors/end users were granted non-exclusive, non-transferable license to use a computer software, this would not constitute royalty.
  - ✓ The Supreme Court stated that it cannot accede to the argument made by the Revenue that the distribution of copyrighted computer software would constitute the grant of an interest in copyright under section 14(b)(ii) of CA, thus necessitating the deduction of tax at source under section 195 of the Act.

- o **Analysis of the term royalty**
  - ✓ The IT Act refers to consideration paid for transfer of all or any rights, including by way of a license, in respect of any copyright, as royalty. Accordingly for a

payment to qualify as royalty under the IT Act, it is imperative that there shall be a transfer of rights in a copyright. A mere sale of software shall not qualify as royalty under the IT Act.

- ✓ As per the DTAA royalty includes payment made for the use or right to use any copyright in a literary work. Even as per the DTAA, sale of software without any transfer of right in copyright will not constitute royalty
- ✓ The following end user license agreements were referred to as illustrative documents:
    - Category 1 – EULA between Samsung Electronics (non-resident supplier) and the end users
    - Category 2A – Re-market agreement between IBM Singapore (non-resident supplier) and IBM India (Indian distributor/ re-marketer
    - Category 2B – EULA with Indian end users of software distributed by IBM India
    - Category 3 – Standard EULAs accompanying Microsoft software products sold to resident Indian end user by Microsoft Corporation (non-resident foreign vendor)
    - Category 4 – Supply contract between Indian company and Swedish supplier (Ericsson Radio Systems AB)
- ✓ On examination of the rights granted to the end users/distributors, the Supreme Court held that the payment made to non-residents did not constitute royalty.
- ✓ The Supreme Court upheld the principle of Copyrighted article versus Copyright and took the view a mere license to use software does not amount to use or license of copyright.

- o **Validity of retrospective Amendment to IT Act**
  - ✓ The definition of "royalty" under the IT Act was amended in 2012 by way of insertion of Explanation 4 (with retrospective effect from June 01, 1976), purportedly to clarify that the transfer of all or any rights in respect of any right, property or information includes right for use/to use a computer software, regardless of the medium through which such right is transferred
  - ✓ Explanation 4 expands the royalty definition. A person who made a payment prior to 2012 cannot be expected to apply the expanded definition of royalty which was not in existence at the time of making payments to determine withholding obligations under section 195.

- Accordingly the Supreme Court held that the amount paid by resident Indian end users/distributors to non-resident computer software manufacturers/suppliers, as consideration for the resale/use of the computer software through EULAs/distribution agreements, is not the payment of royalty for the use of copyright in the computer software, and that the same does not give rise to any income taxable in India, as a result of which the payers (in all four categories referred to in this judgement) were not liable to deduct any TDS under section 195 of the Income Act, 1961.

A detailed below indicates the gist of cases on Permanent Establishment, Taxability of Software before SC ruling and Taxation of Bandwidth Charges[96].

96. Courtesy: My colleague Ankitha Kumari.

1. PE rulings

Sl. No.	Cause Title	Forum	Short description
1	Overseas Transport Co. Ltd	Mumbai Tribunal	Indian agents earning meagre income from Mauritian Shipping co. does not constitute DAPE
2	Mitsui & Co. Ltd	Delhi Tribunal	Mitsui's Indian Subsidiary does not constitute DAPE in India
3	ESPN Star Sports Mauritius S.N.C et Compagnie	Delhi Tribunal	PE determination irrelevant for transactions at ALP between ESPN Group Cos.
4	Bombardier Transportation Sweden AB	Delhi Tribunal	Indian AE fails 'disposal test' for constituting Swedish Co's PE
5	Standard Chartered Grindlays	Delhi Tribunal	Allows FTS deduction to Standard Chartered's Indian PE u/s 37(1), rejects categorisation as 'HO expense' u/s 44C
6	Huawei Technologies Co. Ltd	Delhi Tribunal	Tribunal held that Huawei China bore 'rejection risk' for telecom equipment supply; upheld PE & business connection in India
7	Asia Today Limited	Mumbai Tribunal	Alleged DAPE tax-neutral if Indian agents are remunerated at ALP
8	International Air Transport Association	Mumbai Tribunal	Accredited Training Centres not DAPE of International Air Transport Association under India-Canada DTAA

Sl. No.	Cause Title	Forum	Short description
9	Lubrizol Advanced Materials Inc	Ahmedabad Tribunal	Foreign nationals on deputation exclusively working for Indian AE, not supervisory or agency PE
10	ZTE Corporation	Delhi Tribunal	Tribunal rules on profit attribution, software payments (i.e., held as not taxable)
11	Asia Today Limited	Mumbai Tribunal	Re-domiciliation, no ground to deny DTAA benefits
12	GlaxoSmithKline Asia Pvt. Ltd.	Chandigarh Tribunal	Tribunal remits PE issue under India-Belgium DTAA
13	Telenor ASA	Delhi Tribunal	Interconnected services, provided by Telenor to Unitech, under unified agreement constitutes PE in India

2. Software rulings

Sl. No.	Case law name	Forum	Short description
1	Acer India Private Ltd	Bangalore Tribunal	Acer India not 'assessee-in-default' for TDS non-deduction on software purchase; HC's Samsung ruling inapplicable retrospect-tively
2	Kaseya Software India Private Limited	Bangalore Tribunal	Sec. 195 TDS applicable on software payments to foreign AE, assessee's 'distributor' plea not valid
3	Elsevier BV	AAR	Subscription fee for online scientific database, business income, not royalty

Sl. No.	Case law name	Forum	Short description
4	Barclays Technology Centre India Pvt. Ltd	Pune Tribunal	Subsequent retrospective amendment expanding 'Royalty' scope cannot trigger Sec. 40(a)(ia) disallowance
5	Engineering Analysis Centre of Excellence Private Limited	Supreme Court	Payments for software not taxable as royalty; TDS liability subject to treaty benefits
6	Technicolor India Pvt Ltd and Altisource Business Solutions Private Limited	Karnataka High Court and Bangalore Tribunal	Payments for software not taxable as royalty; SC ruling in Engineering Analysis followed
7	Reliance Corporate IT Park Ltd	Mumbai Tribunal	Payment for software license with restricted use, not Royalty
8	Ansys Inc.	Pune Tribunal	Sale of software/ license not 'royalty'; Business profits sans PE, not taxable
9	QlikTech International AB	Bangalore Tribunal	Tribunal rules out royalty on software sale
10	Kawasaki Microelectronics Inc	Bangalore Tribunal	TDS default on software purchase not bar against depreciation allowance; Tally Solutions followed
11	Infosys Limited	Bangalore Tribunal	Tribunal holds law on 'right to use software' applicable to web-hosting, cloud computing

3. Bandwidth rulings

Sl. No.	Case law name	Forum	Short description
1	Edenred Pte Ltd	Mumbai Tribunal	Receipts for Infrastructure & Data Centre Hosting Services by Singaporean co. not royalty under DTAA
2	Telstra Singapore Pte.Ltd	Delhi Tribunal	Singaporean Co.'s income from bandwidth services, not taxable as royalty
3	Atos Information Technology Singapore Pte Ltd	Mumbai Tribunal	Services provided to subsidiary in India through servers in Singapore, not taxable as Royalty/FTS

4. E-commerce rulings

Sl. No.	Case law name	Forum	Short description
1	Mastercard Asia Pacific Pte. Ltd.	Delhi HC	HC disposes Mastercard's application seeking stay of Equalisation Levy payments
2	LG Electronics India Private Ltd	AAR	Fees paid by LG for advertising, marketing in ICC events, not 'Royalty', PILCOM ruling followed
3	Cloudtail India Private Limited	Delhi HC	HC remands dispute on lower deduction u/s 194-O for Cloudtail India over write-off of slow, ageing inventory
4	Urban Ladder Home Décor Solutions Pvt. Ltd	Bangalore Tribunal	Payments to Facebook, Amazon Web Services for advertising, marketing not taxable as Royalty

ANNEXURES

ANNEXURE 1

COUNTRY-WISE POSITION OF DIGITAL TAXES[97]

Country	Status	Effective date	Nature of levy/ tax	Rate	Applicable tax base	Threshold
Austria	Enacted	January 1, 2020	Digital Services Tax (DST)	5%	Revenues from advertising services on digital interfaces or any type of software or websites rendered in Austria	i) Global turnover of Euro 750M or more, and ii) Turnover in Austria from online advertising services of at least Euro 25M
Belgium	Proposed	-	DST/ Digital PE	3%	Revenues from: 1. Selling advertising space on a digital platform targeted at its users 2. Selling user data gene-rated from user activities on a digital platform 3. Providing digital inter-mediation services to users of a digital platform by facilitating the exchange of supplies of goods or services between those users	Annual worldwide revenues of Euro 750M from digital services activities and national taxable revenues from digital activities of Euro 5M

97. *Source*: https://taxcms.deloitte.com/taxatlasdst; https://tax.kpmg.us/content/dam/tax/en/pdfs/2020/digitalized-economy-taxation-developments-summary.pdf

Country	Status	Effective date	Nature of levy/ tax	Rate	Applicable tax base	Threshold
Brazil	Proposed	-	DST	1% - 3% - 5%	Gross revenue from: 1. Advertising to Brazilian users 2. Making available a digital platform that permits users to interact with the objective of the sale of goods or services directly between such users if one user is located in Brazil 3. Transfer of data from users located in Brazil collected during the use of digital platform or generated by these users	Legal entities domiciled in Brazil or abroad with previous-year global revenues exceeding R$ 3 billion and with gross revenue in Brazil that exceeds R$ 100 million
Canada	Intention	-	DST	3%	Revenues from targeted advertising services and digital intermediation services. Similar to the French DST, so revenues from: 1. Provision of a digital interface enabling users to	Worldwide revenues of the business are at least $1 billion and Canadian revenues are more than $40 million

Country	Status	Effective date	Nature of levy/ tax	Rate	Applicable tax base	Threshold
					enter into contacts and to interact with others ("intermediary services"); and 2. Provision of services to advertisers that aim at placing targeted advertising messages on a digital interface based on data collected about users and generated upon the consultation of such interface ("advertising services based on users data")	
Costa Rica	Enacted	November 19, 2019	General income tax on digital tourist rental services income	NA	Income from provision of tourist rental services via digital platforms	

Country	Status	Effective date	Nature of levy/ tax	Rate	Applicable tax base	Threshold
Czech Republic	Proposed	Expected to be 2021	DST	Originally 7% but now reduced to 5%	Receipts from the following sources: 1. targeted advertising on a digital interface; 2. the transmission of data about users and generated from users' activities on digital interfaces; and 3. the making available to users a multi-sided digital interface which may facilitate the provision of supplies of goods and services among users	Turnover of more than Euro 750M and with a tax base relating to taxable digital services rendered in the CZ exceeding CZK 100 M. Companies whose revenues from digital services do not exceed 10% of total revenues in Europe would be excluded from the DST, but subject to notification duties
European Union	Announced	September 12, 2020	-	-	On July 15, 2020, the EU Commission announced the adoption of a new tax package. One of the initiatives is a proposal to amend the Mutual Assistance Directive	

Country	Status	Effective date	Nature of levy/ tax	Rate	Applicable tax base	Threshold
					on administrative cooperation in the field of taxation (2011/16) to extend the EU tax transparency rules to digital platforms (DAC7). It aims to ensure that member states automatically exchange information on the revenue generated by sellers on online platforms and clarify rules in other areas in which member states work together to fight tax abuse, e.g. through joint tax audits. On September 12, the EU Commission published remarks by Executive Vice-President Valdis Dombrovskis at the informal ECOFIN press conference which indicated that the EU will move ahead with a digital tax proposal if progress is not made at the global level.	

Country	Status	Effective date	Nature of levy/ tax	Rate	Applicable tax base	Threshold
France	Enacted	January 1, 2019 but 2020 DST collection has been delayed to the end of 2020	DST	3%	Portion of taxable services income related to France after application of the "French digital presence" ratios to the corresponding worldwide digital services receipts: 1. Provision of a digital interface enabling users to enter into contacts and to interact with others ("inter-mediary services"). 2. Provision of services to advertisers that aim at placing targeted advertising messages on a digital interface based on data collected about users and generated upon the consultation of such interface ("advertising services based on users' data")	The tax applies only to companies exceeding in the previous taxable year the following thresholds: i) Euro 750M in worldwide revenue and ii) Euro 25M in taxable services supplied in France; these thresholds must be calculated at the consolidated group level.

Country	Status	Effective date	Nature of levy/ tax	Rate	Applicable tax base	Threshold
Greece	Enacted	July 16, 2019	General income tax on digital short-term rental services incomes	NA	Income from short-term rentals in the sharing economy through digital platforms	
Hungary	Enacted	July 1, 2017	DAT	7.5%, although the tax rate reduced to 0%, effective from July 1, 2019 through December 31, 2022	Net turnover for the financial year generated by the broadcasting or publication of advertisements in Hungary	Revenues exceeding HUF 100M per year

Country	Status	Effective date	Nature of levy/ tax	Rate	Applicable tax base	Threshold
India	Enacted	June 1, 2016	Equalisation Levy	6%	Gross amount of online advertising payments from an Indian resident or a non-resident with a permanent establishment to non-residents that lack a PE in India	Payments exceeding INR 100,000 annually
	Enacted	April 1, 2020	Equalisation Levy	2%	1. Online sale of goods owned by the e-commerce operator 2. Online provision of services provided by the e-commerce operator 3. Online sale of goods or provision of services facilitated by the e-commerce operator (i.e., when the operator provides a platform for others to supply goods or provide services) 4. Any combination of the above	The gross receipts/turn-over does not exceed INR 2 crores

Country	Status	Effective date	Nature of levy/ tax	Rate	Applicable tax base	Threshold
	Enacted	October 1, 2020	WHT	1%	Gross amount of sale of goods/ provision of service facilitated through digital or electronic facility or platform	Withholding is not required on payments made to an individual e-commerce participants if their gross amount of sales or services through the e-commerce platform does not exceed INR 0.5 million.
	Enacted	April 1, 2022	Digital PE	-	Revenue related to the digital PE	
Indonesia	Enacted	March 31, 2020	Electronic Transaction Tax	Not decided yet	Imposed on e-commerce sales, when the digital PE cannot be applied due to the provision of a Tax Treaty	
	Enacted	March 31, 2020	Digital PE	NA	Revenue related to the digital PE	
Israel	Intended	Not decided yet	DST	3% or 5%	Not decided yet — it should be modelled on the French DST	
	Enacted	April 12, 2016	Digital PE	NA	Revenue related to the digital PE	

Country	Status	Effective date	Nature of levy/ tax	Rate	Applicable tax base	Threshold
Italy	Enacted	January 1, 2020	DST	3%	Gross revenue derived from: 1. Advertising on a digital interface; 2. A multilateral digital interface that allows users to buy/sell goods and services; and 3. The transmission of user data generated from using a digital interface. When a taxable service is supplied in Italy in a calendar year, the taxable revenue is the percentage of worldwide revenue from digital services that is represented by the services linked to Italy. The determination of the percentage varies based on the category of digital service	The DST applies both to resident and non-resident companies with total revenue in the previous year of at least Euro 750M and total revenue from digital services supplied in Italy of at least Euro 5.5M.

Country	Status	Effective date	Nature of levy/ tax	Rate	Applicable tax base	Threshold
Kenya	Enacted	November 7, 2019	General income tax on digital income	NA	Income accruing through a digital marketplace (i.e., a platform that enables the direct interaction between buyers and sellers of goods and services through electronic means) is chargeable to tax	
Kenya	Enacted	January 1, 2021	DST	1.5%	Gross revenue from digital marketplace	
Latvia	Intended	Not decided yet	DST	3%	Not decided yet — DST revenue (specifics yet to be determined)	
Malaysia	Enacted	May 13, 2019	WHT	Variable	Generally, income tax is imposed on the income of any person accruing in or derived from Malaysia. Any income in relation to e-commerce transactions is deemed to be	

Country	Status	Effective date	Nature of levy/ tax	Rate	Applicable tax base	Threshold
					derived from Malaysia if it is associated with any activities in Malaysia regardless of whether that income is received in Malaysia or otherwise.	
Mexico	Enacted	June 1, 2020	WHT	Variable	Payments for non-residents for certain digital services such as downloads or access to images, movies, text, information, video, audio, music, games (including gambling), other multimedia content, multi-player environments, mobile tones, online news, traffic information, weather forecasts and statistics, online clubs, dating websites, long-distance teaching or testing	

Country	Status	Effective date	Nature of levy/ tax	Rate	Applicable tax base	Threshold
Nigeria	Enacted	February 3, 2020	Digital PE	NA	Revenue related to the digital PE. Non-resident company will have an SEP in Nigeria if it has gross turnover or income beyond threshold from four types of digital activities: 1. providing streaming or downloading services of digital content, such as movies, music, games, and e-books to persons in Nigeria; 2. transmitting data collected on Nigerian user activities on a digital interface, such as websites or apps; 3. providing goods and services directly or indirectly through a digital platform; or 4. providing intermediary services via a digital platform, website, or app linking suppliers to customers in the Nigerian market.	Gross turnover or income of more than NGN 25 million

Country	Status	Effective date	Nature of levy/ tax	Rate	Applicable tax base	Threshold
					A foreign company will also have an SEP if it uses a Nigerian domain name or has a URL registered in Nigeria, or if it has a "purposeful and sustained interaction with persons in Nigeria by customising its digital page or platform" for the Nigerian market. Customisation includes providing prices for products or services in Nigerian currency or offering payment or billing options in Nigerian currency.	
Pakistan	Enacted	July 1, 2018	WHT	5%	Payments for offshore digital services (such as online advertising, designing, creating, hosting or maintenance of websites, providing any facility or service for uploading, storing	

Country	Status	Effective date	Nature of levy/ tax	Rate	Applicable tax base	Threshold
					or distribution of digital content, online collection or processing of data related to users in Pakistan, any facility for online sale of goods or services, or any other online facility) performed by non-resident persons	
Paraguay	Enacted	January 1, 2021	Non-resident Tax (INR)	15%	Income net of VAT from the provision of digital services by foreign suppliers	
Poland	Enacted	July 1, 2020	DST	1.5%	Gross revenue of on demand provider resulting from: 1. access to audio-visual media service, and 2. audio-visual commercial communication	
OECD	Announced	September 15, 2020	-	-	The OECD update states that, despite Covid-19, it has been able to lead development of technical aspects on the two-pillar approach and reports on	

Country	Status	Effective date	Nature of levy/ tax	Rate	Applicable tax base	Threshold
					the blueprint for each pillar; once finalised, it will be placed for inclusive framework comments along with other reports such as impact assessment. OECD has released model rules for reporting by platform operators with respect to sellers in the sharing and gig economy. Under these rules, the onus of collecting information and passing it to the tax authorities is on platform providers. The information is required for those sellers/service providers who provide accommodation, transport and personal services.	
Slovakia	Enacted	January 1, 2018	WHT	5%	Payments to foreign digital platforms facilitating transport and lodging services in Slovakia, acting as a marketplace for such services	

Country	Status	Effective date	Nature of levy/ tax	Rate	Applicable tax base	Threshold
					in Slovakia, not registered as a PE in Slovakia	
Spain	Proposed	Not decided yet	DST	3%	Gross revenue from online advertising services, the sale of online advertising and the sale of user- data	Companies with a global net turnover exceeding Euro 750M and with total revenues from taxable provision of digital services exceeding Euro 3M in Spain
Taiwan	Enacted	January 1, 2017	WHT	To be agreed with the tax authority	Payments to foreign providers for online advertisement and remunerations for e-services, such as online games, videos, audio broadcast, movie, TV series, music and online platform services	
Thailand	Proposed	TBD	WHT	5%	Income from e-commerce supplies of goods and services in the country, including online advertising, gaming, shopping, and others	

Country	Status	Effective date	Nature of levy/ tax	Rate	Applicable tax base	Threshold
Tunisia	Enacted	January 1, 2020	DST	3%	Applies on the sale of computer applications and digital services by non-resident companies. Detailed requirement to be determined by decree	
	Enacted	January 1, 2019	WHT	15%	Payments made to providers of advertising services or intermediaries in return for the provision of such services via the internet	
Turkey	Enacted	March 1, 2020	DST	7.5% but the President can reduce to 1% or increase to 15%	Gross revenue derived from in scope services (i.e., digital advertising services, sales of any audible, visual or digital content, services for the provision and operation of a digital platform by which users may interact with each other). No deductions would be available for expenses, costs or tax	Revenue derived from digital services exceeding TRY 20,000,000 (approx. Euro 3.14M) in Turkey and Euro 750M (or equivalent) worldwide

Country	Status	Effective date	Nature of levy/ tax	Rate	Applicable tax base	Threshold
United Kingdom	Enacted	April 1, 2020	DST	2%	Revenue derived from UK users from three types of digital activities: 1. Social media platforms 2. Internet search engine 3. Online marketplace	A group's worldwide revenues from these digital activities are more than £500M and more than £25M of these revenues are derived from UK users
Uruguay	Enacted	January 1, 2018	General income tax on digital services income	NA	Income of non-residents from services related to businesses involved in the digital economy in Uruguay	
United Nations	Proposed	September 1, 2020	-	-	The UN released a draft proposal giving source countries the right to tax cross-border payments for automated digital services via a with-holding tax on gross income or an apportionment formula on net income. The automated digital services within this scope are online advertising	

Country	Status	Effective date	Nature of levy/ tax	Rate	Applicable tax base	Threshold
					services, online intermediation platform services, social media services, digital content services, Cloud computing services, sale or other alienation of user data, and standardised online teaching services.	
United States	Announced	September 1, 2020	-	-	The U.S. has expressed strongly opposed the imposition of digital services taxes by various countries, considering it as a discrimination against U.S. companies. On July 22, 2020, the Office of the U.S. Trade Representative (USTR) announced that it has initiated investigations of digital services taxes that have been adopted or are being considered by certain trading partners of the United States (this list includes India)	

Country	Status	Effective date	Nature of levy/ tax	Rate	Applicable tax base	Threshold
Vietnam	Enacted	January 1, 2021	WHT	Variable	Income derived by non-residents from digital and e-commerce operations in Vietnam	
Zimbabwe	Enacted	January 1, 2019	General income tax on certain digital services income	5%	Any amount receivable by or on behalf of an e-commerce platform/satellite broadcasting service provider domiciled outside Zimbabwe from persons resident in Zimbabwe	Revenue exceeds USD 500,000 per annum.

ANNEXURE 2

INDICATORS FOR ADS & CFB

Summary of revenue sourcing rules and acceptable indicators for Consumer Facing Businesses (CFB)

Revenue streams	Sourcing rule	Relevant Indicators per revenue indicator*
- Revenue from consumer-facing goods sold directly to consumer	The jurisdiction of the place of final delivery of the good to the consumer.	a) The jurisdiction of the retail storefront directly selling to consumers; or if not applicable b) The jurisdiction of the final delivery address of the goods to the consumer
- Revenue from consumer-facing goods sold through Independent Distributor	The jurisdiction of the place of final delivery of the good to the consumer.	a) The jurisdiction of the place of final delivery to the consumer as reported by the independent distributor, based on:- i. The jurisdiction of the retail storefront directly selling to consumers; or if not applicable ii. The jurisdiction of the final delivery address of the goods; or if unavailable

Revenue streams	Sourcing rule	Relevant Indicators per revenue indicator*
		b) The jurisdiction of the place of final delivery of the good to the consumer as indicated by other information already available to the MNE.
- Revenue from consumer-facing services	The jurisdiction of the place of enjoyment or use of the service.	a) The jurisdiction of the address where the service is performed; or b) For services delivered online, the jurisdiction of the ordinary residence of the user, based on:- i. The jurisdiction of the ordinary residence of the purchaser based on user profile information**; or if unavailable or unreliable ii. The jurisdiction of the billing address of the purchaser; or if unavailable or unreliable iii. The jurisdiction of the geolocation of the device of the purchaser; or if unavailable or unreliable iv. The jurisdiction of the IP address of the device of the purchase.

Revenue streams	Sourcing rule	Relevant Indicators per revenue indicator*
- Revenue from franchising and licensing	<u>**(i) Consumer-facing goods**</u> For revenue from franchising goods or licensing an intangible that is attached to goods is the jurisdiction of the place of final delivery of the good to the consumer.	a) The jurisdiction of the place of delivery or enjoyment as reported by the franchisee or licensee, based on:- i. The jurisdiction of the retail storefront directly selling to consumers; or if not applicable ii. The jurisdiction of the final delivery address of the goods; or if unavailable b) The jurisdiction of the place of final delivery of the good to the consumer as indicated by other information already available to franchisor / licensor
	<u>**(i) Consumer-facing services**</u> For revenue from franchising services or licensing an intangible that is used to support the provision of a service to consumers is the jurisdiction of the place of enjoyment or use of the service.	a) The jurisdiction of the place of delivery or enjoyment as reported by the franchisee or licensee, based on:- i. The jurisdiction of the address where the service is performed; or if unavailable

Revenue streams	Sourcing rule	Relevant Indicators per revenue indicator*
		b) The jurisdiction of the place of enjoyment or use of the service as indicated by other information already available to franchisor/licensor

Note

**** An MNE will apply the indicator that appears first in the hierarchy of indicators, unless this information is unavailable or unreliable as noted within each rule.***

***** The user profile information is as follows:***

- *i. Information on residence obtained from recurring data on geolocation or IP address of the purchaser's device; or if unavailable or unreliable*
- *ii. Billing address of the purchaser; or if unavailable or unreliable*
- *iii. Mobile country code of the phone number of the purchaser; or if unavailable or unreliable*
- *iv. Information on residence inputted by the purchaser; or if unavailable or unreliable*
- *v. Other available information that can be used to determine the jurisdiction of the ordinary residence of the purchaser; or if unavailable or unreliable*

Subject Index

D